THE PEOPLE'S C.
Film and the Co-operative Movement

By Alan Burton

Published by the National Film Theatre, 1994

Design and production by Nic
Design concept by Thumb D(
Printed by KPC Group, Lond

The National Film Theatre is a division of
the British Film Institute

Director: Wilf Stevenson
Controller BFI South Bank: Adrian Wootton
Acting Head of Programme Planning: Mark Adams

National Film Theatre
South Bank, Waterloo
London, SE1 8XT
© National Film Theatre, 1994
ISBN 0-85170-491-3

NFT Programme Planning Staff:
Acting Deputy Head of Programme Planning: John Mount
Assistant to Acting Head of Programme Planning: Hilary Smith
Programme Co-ordinator: Julie Pearce
Assistant Programme Co-ordinator: Heather Osborn
Assistant: Dayle Hodgson
Special Events: Maggi Hurt
Programme Research: John Gillett
Programme Notes Production: Vicki Cottis
Print and Design: Nicola Woodford
Booklet Co-ordinator: Rita Foreman

bfi
CELEBRATING THE MOVING IMAGE

The British Film Institute exists to encourage the development of film, television and video in the United Kingdom, and to promote knowledge, understanding and enjoyment of the culture of the moving image. Its activities include the National Film Archive; The National Film Theatre; The London Film Festival; The Museum of the Moving Image; the production and distribution of film and video; Library and Information Services; Stills, Posters and Designs; Research; Publishing and Education; and the monthly *Sight and Sound* magazine.

CONTENTS

Foreword, by Lord Attenborough	8
Introduction	10
The CWS: Providing a Film Service for the Movement	18
Joseph Reeves: Films for Education and Social Change	40
FHW Cox: Films for Propaganda and Political Change	52
JH Poyser: Local Co-operative Films	64
Horace Masterman and Co-operative Cinemas	74
Conclusion	84
Bibliography	86

ACKNOWLEDGEMENTS

Despite the convention of an individual name appearing on the cover, a book is invariably the result of co–operation, and involves varied levels of contribution from many. This present project is certainly no exception. The establishment of the National Co–operative Film Archive in 1992, by the Member Education Department of the Co–operative Union Ltd, at the International Co–operative College in Leicestershire, provided the initial impetus, and the necessary resources, to commence the task of researching the co–operative movement and film. The desire to celebrate the achievements of 150 years of co–operation since the founding of the Rochdale Equitable Pioneers' Society, with a Festival of Films on Co–operation, provided the specific opportunity to record that history.

I would like to take this opportunity to record my grateful thanks to those numerous colleagues, friends, historians and archivists, who were instrumental in the preparation of this volume. Foremost is Mervyn Wilson, Officer for Member Education at the International Co–operative College, who always believed in the overall project and was prepared to make funds available from limited resources, to allow the Film Archive, and the attendant research, to progress. A special tribute must go to the secretarial staff of the Co–operative College, who had to put up with my bruising deadlines, and total absence of typing skills.

Many co–operative 'historians' within the movement have patiently listened to my ideas and provided invaluable suggestions. All film historians are of course beholden to those un–sung heroes who continue to make available the raw material of cinema history, the film archivists. The historian of the 'alternative', or marginal cinema, is especially in their debt, as precious little funding is available to preserve such titles. Particular gratitude must therefore be expressed to the staffs of the East Anglian Film Archive, Scottish Film Archive, North West Film Archive, Northern Film and Television Archive, Wessex Sound and Film Archive, Educational and Television Films Ltd and the National Film and Television Archive. My thanks also go to the staffs of the Co–operative Union Libraries, the CWS Library, the TUC Library, the Working Class History Library, and the British Film Institute Library.

Finally, I would like to record my thanks to Deac Rossell, who first proposed the idea of this study, Professor Jeffrey Richards who has provided so much inspiration to all students of cinema history, to Sandra Hebron and Cornerhouse, to Mark Adams and the NFT, to The Cinema Theatre Association and The Mercia Cinema Society. Most of all to Sue Pascoe, who always exhibited more faith than myself in my ability to complete the project.

The 1994 Festival of Films on Co–operation has provided a unique opportunity to bring before the public a 'lost' fragment of film history, and ensure the continued availability of those 'people's' films for posterity.

Alan Burton
Junior Research Fellow in Media Studies, De Montfort University, and Consultant, National Co-operative Film Archive.

The National Co-operative Film Archive was established in 1992 with funding provided by the National Co-operative Education Association. It aims to preserve all film and photographic material relating to the consumer co-operative movement, to promote the use of archive films in co-operative education and to stimulte research into the movement's use of film.

This project has been made possible with generous funding from the Co-operative Movement's 150th anniversary celebrations committee.

The Co-operative Movement continues its association with film-making through its sponsorship of the Young People's Film and Video Festival. The Festival commenced in 1966 under the auspices of the London Co-operative Society and is now organised by Co-operative Retail Services Ltd, with the annual screenings alternating between the National Film Theatre and the National Museum of Photography, Film and TV in Bradford. It remains a premier showcase for young talent and emphasises the collaborative aspects of film-making rather than the competitive. The co-operative principle remains paramount in the independent film sector, where the thrust of socially aware film-making is to be found today. I would like to acknowledge the achievements and social commitment of this sector, which carries on a great tradition.

FOREWORD

By Lord Attenborough

December 21 1844 is not a date which history students strive to memorise, yet its significance in the cannon of events affecting the lives of ordinary people is great indeed. On that day 150 years ago, a group of impoverished Lancashire weavers banded together to form the Rochdale Equitable Pioneers' Society. Inspired by ideals of self-help, mutuality and co-operation, their new business venture prospered and offered new hope to working people everywhere. Today over 800 million people around the world co-operate together in numerous businesses, jointly contributing and taking decisions for the benefit of all. Throughout 1994 they will be celebrating a century and a half of achievement.

Most people who lived in Britain during the inter-war and post-war period had some contact with the local 'Co-op'. For many it meant involvement in community activities and co-operative society affairs. But the most significant factor for those of slender means was undoubtedly the termly 'divi' when a proportion of what they had spent at the local Co-op shop was returned in the form of credit. Many will recall their mother buying them a pair of shoes or a new coat on 'divi day'. Some will still be able to recite their family's 'divi' number which had to be quoted on each and every errand to the local shop.

I am proud of my own family's involvement with the Co-op. Both my parents were members in Leicester and my grandfather helped form a Midland Co-operative Society. By the late 1940s, I personally was involved in a variety of co-operative activities which ranged from giving talks on film acting and production to members and staff of the London Co-operative Society, promoting Co-operative Wholesale Society products such as the celebrated 'Defiant Radio' and adjudicating contests for the annual 'Co-operative Queen'.

The Co-operative Film Festival, which is to tour venues up and down the country following its launch in August 1994, will provide a welcome opportunity to take a look, once again, at the triumphs of the co-operative movement and to appreciate the real benefits to the co-operators themselves.

Films were used for a variety of purposes within the movement. Some were shown in cinemas to publicise co-operative products, such as the celebrated tea. Others sought to persuade audiences to become active members of their local society. Where they had the skills and equipment, members often made films themselves, producing 'news reels' of significant society events and co-operative activities. Film shows were mounted to instruct existing members in the ideals, history and workings of their great movement, or sometimes simply to provide recreation and entertainment during their leisure hours. The highlight of this dedicated activity was the production, to mark the centenary of the movement in 1944, of a fifty-minute feature film, *Men of Rochdale*, by the Co-op's own film unit. This recounted the trials, ultimate triumph and vital legacy of the pioneer co-operators. Because it was made at the end of the Second World War and projected a stimulating sense of optimism, the film was far more than a history lesson and also recognised that although much had been achieved, still more needed to be done. Such ideals and commitment remain, of course, fitting examples for the world of 1994.

The Festival of Films on Co-operation includes historic films of local and national co-operative activities and the fascinating dossier which follows provides a detailed study of their production and exhibition, demonstrating how readily co-operators embraced film-making in their crusade to create the 'Co-operative Commonwealth'.

Picture shows Lord Attenborough and his wife Sheila Sim promoting a Co-op 'Defiant' television in 1949.

INTRODUCTION

Narrator (George Jacob Holyoake):
'Men of Rochdale are you satisfied?
William Cooper what have you to say?'

William Cooper:
'I was a socialist. We socialists wanted to make a city of brotherhood, a city of light set on a hill for all to see.
A city free from poverty, crime, and meanness.
Is there such a city yet?'

Narrator: *'Not yet William Cooper'.*

William Cooper:
'Then our work is not yet done.
Are there men in England left to do it?'

Narrator: *'Yes, William Cooper. There are men still to be found. Men who seek the Co–operative way of life. Men who will finish the work you men of Rochdale started.'*

[End sequence to *Men of Rochdale* (1944)]

Men of Rochdale was made by the Co–operative Wholesale Society (CWS) film unit in 1944, the centenary year of the Rochdale Equitable Pioneers' Society, and generally accepted as the centenary of the co–operative movement. Despite the restrictions imposed by war–time conditions, the movement was adamant that its achievements would not pass unrecognised. The film, budgeted at a healthy £15,000, was co–produced by the CWS and Sidney Box, a producer long associated with the CWS through his involvement with Publicity Films Ltd., which first produced CWS promotional films in 1928. Following the production he made a remarkably successful transfer to the feature film industry.[1]

INTRODUCTION

Men of Rochdale (1944): 1851 and the Pioneers face a crisis of insolvency due to malicious rumours spread by local tradesmen

The exchange on the facing page is the culmination of the film. The original Rochdale Pioneers, represented here by Miles Ashworth, James Standring, James Smithies, Charles Haworth and William Cooper, superimposed over sky and cloud, survey the contemporary world. At the prompting of that great 19th century co–operator and historian of the movement, George Jacob Holyoake, they declare their dissatisfaction with the progress towards the 'Co–operative Commonwealth'. The film thus exhorts co–operators to continue the fight against the injustices of war and capitalism, 'work and war for the profit of others', and the scene is particularly resonant of the immediate post–Beveridge period. At that time even the commercial film industry flirted with such sentiment, as in Ealing's adaptation of JB Priestley's *They Came To A City* (1944). Not surprisingly, there was much rejoicing following Labour's landslide victory in the General Election of July 1945.[2]

The co–operative movement's involvement in film–making follows the general contours of film history in Britain. Short films of CWS factories became an integral part of the magic lantern lecture programme as early as 1898 [3], two years after the first public screenings of moving pictures in London. Such lectures were a traditional aspect of the educational and cultural activities sponsored by societies, giving their members the opportunity to meet, to discuss issues and consider developments, as well as enjoy an evening of song, dance and entertainment in the spirit of the co–operative community. The first films commissioned by the CWS 'showed views of their soap, starch and candleworks at Irlam, their biscuit factory at Crumsall (sic) and the tea warehouses of the English and Scottish Joint Co–operative Wholesale Society in London'.[4] The movement's use of film would expand considerably following those tentative beginnings, and would more fully embrace its training, publicity, educational and propaganda requirements. An extensive programme of film exhibition, utilising mobile units on a road show basis, was maintained by the CWS until the mid–1960s. Changing recreational patterns and technology, which had brought about a dramatic down–turn in business for the commercial industry, also put paid to the CWS' cinema activities, and significantly the film unit of the CWS Publicity Department was disbanded in 1966.

CWS Tea Demonstration Van 1935: equipped to give promotional sound film demonstrations

INTRODUCTION

Film star Carl Brisson at a Co-op mobile shop, 1931

The following historical survey is concerned with the consumer co–operative movement and its use of film during the seven decades after 1898. The movement was essentially a grouping of individual co–operative societies, each trading in a geographically defined region, which together owned and controlled the CWS, the main procurer and manufacturer of Co–op brand products. Societies were further federated into the Co–operative Union, a body providing specialist services to societies, and acting as spokesperson for the movement. Other important groups within the movement were the Co–operative Women's Guild (formerly Women's Co–operative Guild) and young people's organisations such as the British Federation of Co–operative Youth and the Woodcraft Folk. Although 'outside' of the consumer movement, the Co–operative Productive Federation, concerned with workers' co–operation, was in ideological empathy with its larger relation, and was also engaged in film activity in the 1930s.

By the inter–war period the Co–op was a key retailer and 'the CWS was one of the largest concerns in the British food and consumer industry'.[5] It was soon understood that film had a role to play in those commercial activities, and, for the CWS in particular, film was appreciated for its promotional, advertising and publicity value. Further, by the later 1930s, film as a training medium had been explored and was beginning to be exploited. As a large commercial organisation such uses were to be expected. However, as an organisation dependent on voluntary membership, functioning through democratic participation and ideologically driven, advocates were soon promoting film for educational, cultural and propaganda purposes. The historian must be careful not to place a too schematic evaluation on the uses to which film was put. The nature of co-operative philosophy was such that the promotion of the trading activities of the movement was itself a political statement. The co-operative movement was anti-capitalist, in that it dispensed with competition and profit and rather advocated 'production for use' by, and for, all consumers. That was predicated on the return of profits to the consumer-members in the form of dividends. Even today, popular memories of the Co-op are invariably associated with the almost mythical status of 'the divi'. Therefore a publicity film promoting, for instance, CWS Pelaw Polishes, was ideologically determined (as are advertisements promoting the products of capitalist industry), and through promotion, education and entertainment, was making its own small contribution to the realisation of the 'Co-operative Commonwealth'.

For the active co-operator the culture of co-operation could be all-embracing. As a constituent part of the wider labour movement, the Co-op offered its membership a full outlet for their political, cultural and recreational energies and ambitions. Most societies entertained branches of the Co-operative Party (founded 1917), and, through the programmes of their education committees, supported a variety of cultural and recreational activities. The movement was active in the various cultural organisations promoted by the Left such as the Workers' Travel Association and the Workers' Music Association, and, in addition, societies directly sponsored their own drama groups, cycling clubs, brass bands, choirs, youth organisations, holiday camps and Men's, Women's and Mixed Guilds etc. Such cultural formations were essentially 'alternative' to varieties promoted by the dominant ideology, and on occasion 'oppositional', directly confronting that ideology and seeking to change society.[6] Within that cultural framework film made a distinct contribution to the challenge against the dominant order.[7]

Throughout its history the co-operative movement attracted virulent attacks, ranging from the small trader who witnessed his working-class customers transfer their patronage to the Co-op, through to press barons like Lord Beaverbrook, who during the early-mid 1930s marshalled his organs of the mass media against co-operative trading.[8] The 'Defiant' Radio was triumphantly marketed by the CWS after it had broken a boycott imposed on them by the Radio Manufacturers' Association,[9]

'Whilst Co-operative wireless sets for co-operative broadcasts' became the slogan adopted in the long-running campaign against what was felt to be bias promoted by the BBC in their dealings with the movement. It was felt that a media controlled by capitalism was bound to be prejudiced to the labour movement, and that assumption lay behind the formation of the workers' film movement in the late 1920s.[10]

As a large commercial organisation, the co-operative movement intersected with the dominant mass-media, the cinema, in a number of obvious ways. For instance film stars were used in promotional activities to endorse products. The most notable example was the participation of Gracie Fields, undoubtably Britain's most popular performer, between the late 1920s and World War II. 'Our Gracie' and 'T'Co-op' were Rochdale's two greatest gifts to the world, and the celebrity performer gained considerable publicity visiting local co-operative stores and exhibitions as she toured the country.[11] Other film personalities thus engaged included: Carl Brisson; Petula Clark; Kathleen Harrison; George Formby; Margaret Lockwood; Leslie Banks; John Mills; Jimmy Hanley; Rosamund John and Richard Attenborough.

Gracie Fields promoting Scottish CWS salmon, 1938

The movement held varied, sometimes contradictory, attitudes to the cinema, itself by no means exceptional within the labour movement. As Stephen Jones has argued, three general perspectives are identifiable; Moralist; Libertarian; and Marxist, all identifiable with respect to the co–operative movement. The Co–operative Women's Guild often expressed concern over the 'Bad influence of Amusement Palaces', especially on young people, whilst in 1928 it campaigned against the 'Menace of the War Films'.[13] For some co-operative critics the cinema was 'culturally rootless', and their elitist mission became one of 'improvement'.[14] In direct contrast the libertarian position appreciated cinema–going as the perfectly acceptable leisure choice of the working family, for whom 'the cinema offers a pleasing contrast to life as it really is'.[15] In a general way, issues relating to cinema, its development, and its influence, were continually debated within the movement, and articles regularly appeared on such matters as the education film, recent legislation, censorship, criticism, 'How Films are Made', nationalisation, documentary, Hollywood's domination etc. The co–operative movement failed to develop a body of theory regarding the cinema, as systematic as that of the communists.[16] However, as we shall see, much of the movement's actual response was determined by its desire to confront the capitalist ideology of the commercial cinema. An 'alternative' co–operative cinema, alongside the other workers' cinemas of the inter–war period, was directly perceived as a challenge to the cultural and commercial hegemony.

The following study examines five specific areas of activity, beginning with a survey of the leading provider of films to the movement, the CWS. Each subsequent chapter, for means of narrative efficiency, takes as its focus an individual co–operative activist who made a vital contribution to co–operative film–making and exhibition. All of the individuals concerned would readily have acknowledged the necessary assistance and involvement of others. After all, film–making is often recognised as the most collaborative of all art forms. That said, what follows is my personal testimony to Joseph Reeves, Frank Cox, JH Poyser and Horace Masterman, co–operators and film–makers.

NOTES

[1] See BOX, M (1974) Odd Woman Out (London) Ch 12.

[2] For a general history of the Administration see MORGAN, KO (1984) Labour in Power 1945–51 (Oxford).

[3] REDFERN, P (1938) The New History of the CWS (London). Sidney Box suggests the first CWS films were produced a year later in 1899. See BOX, S (1936) 'Britain's First Advertising Films Were Shown in 1899' in The Commercial Film, March, p6.

[4] 'Britain's First Advertising Films', op cit. p6.

[5] JONES, SG (1987) The British Labour Movement and Film, 1918–1939 (London) p150–151.

[6] See JONES, SG (1986) Workers at Play. A Social and Economic History of Leisure, 1918–39 (London) Ch 6.

[7] See bibliography.

[8] See KILLINGBACK, N (1988) 'Limits to Mutuality: Economic and Political Attacks on Co–operation During the 1920s and 1930s' in YEO, S. (ed) (1988) New Views of Co–operation (London). The Co–operative News carried many editorials devoted to the campaign. See for instance Co–operative News, 3 February, 1934, p2.; Co–operative News, 17 February, 1934, p2 and p5.; Co–operative News, 14 April, 1934, p2.

[9] Co–operative News, 28 January, 1933, p1.; Co–operative News, 13 January, 1934, p1.; Co–operative News, 18 August, 1934, p2.

[10] See bibliography.

[11] Co–operative News, 27 December, 1930, p5.; Co–operative News, 17 January, 1931, p5.; Co–operative News, 20 August, 1938, p1.; Co–operative News, 29 October, 1949, p1. Gracie Fields produced a 'hit' record in the late 1920s with 'Shopping at the Co–op Shop'.

[12] The British Labour Movement and Film, op cit. pp 39–58.

[13] Co–operative News, 14 March, 1942, p12; Co–operative News, 14 January, 1928, p12. As a leading advocate of peace the latter position is understandable.

[14] STOCKS, M (1950) 'Creating a Taste for Films' in Co–operative News, 25 February, pp 8–9.

[15] Co–operative News, 8 December, 1934, p11.

[16] For original articles from the 1930s see MACPHERSON, D (1980) Traditions of Independence (London).

THE CWS: PROVIDING A FILM SERVICE FOR THE MOVEMENT

The Co-operative Wholesale Society (CWS) was established by retail co-operative societies in 1863 and began trading in March 1864. The first retail co-operative societies had been formed to protect their members from the adulterated produce purveyed by private traders, and, in a similar manner, the CWS offered a safeguard from unscrupulous suppliers. Furthermore, the extension of co-operation to wholesaling helped stem the flow of working people's resources to the 'middle–man', considered, by many co–operators and socialists, a particularly repugnant form of profit–taking. The principle of consumer self–supply soon extended beyond retailing and wholesaling to embrace direct production, and such services as shipping, publishing, printing, banking, building and insurance, were all successfully undertaken by the CWS before the First World War.

Centralised publicity was an important responsibility of the CWS, and as previously argued, co-operative publicity could not be limited to the selling of goods and services. As Percy Redfern has suggested: 'To inform co–operators and to sell CWS goods are aims that, in CWS history, always have been twins'.[1] We have seen that magic–lantern lectures were a traditional form of educational/publicity activity, and one significant series of lectures detailed the extent and nature of the CWS's productive works, for which lantern slides were specially commissioned.[2] When technology allowed, 'moving pictures' of CWS productions were cast alongside those 'frozen' images, providing a more dynamic dimension to the lecture programme. In this respect, the CWS was undoubtedly a pioneer in the use of industrial films.

Looking back on that early period from the perspective of the mid–1930s, The Commercial Film observed:

> It is worth noting that they (the CWS) helped to popularise the cinema as it is understood today, by taking films into hundreds of towns and villages, particularly in the north of England where they had never been seen before. Many villages which still have no cinema have had regular shows of CWS films.[3]

Such a show was given at Darlington in the spring of 1902. The 'cinematograph entertainment', given under the auspices of the education committee, was provided by the CWS Department at Newcastle. The Co-operative News records that 'the building was packed to excess by an appreciative audience who greatly admired the various places of business and workshops belonging to the Co-operative Wholesale Society'.[4]

The available technology determined that the initial films would be short (25/50ft – approx 1 minute). However, the CWS kept abreast of technical developments, and in the winter of 1903/4 a new Gaumont camera and projector were purchased, allowing for individual film presentations of 150ft (approx 3 minutes), by the Society's two full–time projectionists. Films offering more detailed examinations of CWS factories were now screened in popular film–shows, which also included travel and comedy subjects, thus broadening the appeal of the publicity activity. The silent CWS films of the period had no titles and, in the manner of the lantern lecture, 'a running commentary explaining the shots thrown on the screen was provided by the projectionist as he showed the film. This was no mean feat either, since all machines at this time were manipulated by hand'.[5]

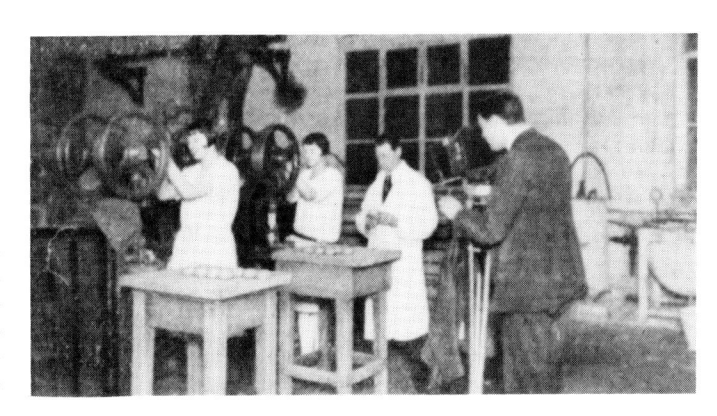

Filming at the Irlam Soap Works for the first CWS story film The Magic Basket (1928)

The CWS Mobile Daylight Cinema giving 'propaganda' film shows outside a Birkenhead polling station on Election Day 1950

The typical venues for CWS filmshows were co-operative and village halls, churches and chapels, with a number taking place in the open air. Up to 1914 almost all of the CWS factories were filmed and a library of 40 films was compiled. Individual films were now being given their own titles and lasting up to 1,000ft (approx 20 minutes).

A typical lecture evening continued to combine lantern views and moving pictures. Such an address was given to the Congleton Society on 14 October 1913, by 'Mr F C Crowther (CWS Manchester), in his lecture on "The CWS and Its Work" illustrated by lantern and cinematograph films' which 'showed goods manufactured by the CWS from the raw material to the finished article'. The Chairman of the Education Committee took the opportunity to impress upon members the need for loyalty to their own society and the CWS, thus demonstrating the perceived 'propaganda' value of the events. Furthermore, marketing opportunities were not ignored, and 'at the conclusion of the lecture, samples of CWS productions were distributed free'.[6] As we shall see, the combination of education, publicity and marketing (in the parlance of the time, 'propaganda') would continue to motivate the co-operative film shows and undergoing further refinements such as the special preparation of films for particular campaigns.

By the eve of the First World War the co-operative movement had developed a comparatively sophisticated appreciation of film, and the potential of the new medium was becoming widely discussed in the movement. In February 1914 the Co-operative News carried a special editorial on 'The Cinema', and debated 'Should It Be Used For Co-operative Purposes?' The article was unequivocal in its praise, and suggested:

> That the cinema might be used, with much advantage for spreading a knowledge of co-operative activities. We are always looking about us for features that will not only bring people into our ranks, but that disseminate information about our great undertakings and, by that means, convey something of the extent of our operations and their possibilities in the near and distant future. Why not bring the cinema to aid?

The anonymous writer understood the unique visual appeal of cinema and the attendant advantages it held for the general public over written propaganda, in arguing that:

> The great advantage to us would be its spread of a knowledge of co-operative activities in the way that the rank and file of

the movement would come to see and learn. We are always talking about the necessity of reaching the masses and bringing the masses together. The cinema would do this for us.[7]

The following month a lecture on 'The Camera as Educator' was delivered at Holyoake House, the headquarters of the Co-operative Union. Here Mr T Simmons advocated the extension of 'the educational activities of the movement through the camera and the cinematograph'. The ideological dimension of his understanding of co-operative education was apparent, when 'he threw on the screen illustrations of the CWS factories, at the same time appealing to his audience to support the productions of these factories, *and thus aim a decisive blow at the sweated industries*'.[8]

The outbreak of war made an unwelcome intervention into that discourse, and further significant advances in the use of film by the movement would not be realised for over a decade. However, it must not be forgotten that the First World War brought fundamental changes in the status of the labour movement and that the post–war world offered an altered economic and political environment in which to operate.[9] One response by the co-operative movement to those changing circumstances, albeit an important one, was to formally enter the political arena with the establishment of the Parliamentary Committee of Congress (later Co-operative Party) in 1917.[10]

In 1916 the CWS had decided on the establishment of a specific publicity department to co–ordinate the burgeoning promotional activities. In the immediate post–war period the department largely concerned itself with print media, concentrating on the launch of a new trade journal, The Producer and Consumer, for instance. CWS film work does not appear to have developed beyond the pattern of the pre–war period, with films of CWS productions screened largely to member audiences, and serving as illustrations to traditional verbal presentations. An interesting departure to that convention was enacted at the British Empire Exhibition in 1925. The CWS was represented at the 'Palace of Industry' and had innovatively secured a nearby 'Picture Palace', where free shows of CWS films were given several times daily. Such a strategy led the Co–op beyond typical criticisms of preaching to the converted, and it was reported that 'Altogether the entertainment is of an educational character and should prove advantageous in making known to many non–members the wide extent of the productive

> **SEE THESE CWS FILMS WHEN THEY COME TO YOUR CINEMA**
>
> **"WORK AND PLAY"**
> THE C.W.S. WELFARE FILM.
> WEEK COMMENCING NOVEMBER 10th.
>
> Invicta Cinema, Chatham.
> Pavilion, Treorchy.
> New Garden Cinema, Bewdley.
> Osborne Cinema, Cheadle.
> Empress Picture House, Urmston.
> Carlton Picture House, Goole.
> King's Cliff Cinema, Brighton.
> Regent Palace, Finedon.
> Victoria Picture House, Littleborough.
> Grand Cinema, Great Harwood.
> Oxford Hall, Keighley.
> Premier, Tanshelf (Pontefract).
> Central Cinema, Tooting, S.W.
> Crown Cinema, Bicester.
> Albion Picture Theatre, Handsworth.
> Queen's Palace Cinema, Silverdale.
> Central Cinema, Blackfords (Cannock).
> Co-operative Hall, Langwith.
>
> Coliseum Electric, Northampton.
> Victory Cinema, Horncastle.
> Empire Music Hall, Liverpool.
> Pavilion, Sankey Green, Warrington.
> Salthouse Pavilion, Barrow-in-Furness.
> Queen's Electric Cinema, Ashton-under-Lyne.
> Picture Palace, Guiseley (Leeds).
> Empire Music Hall, Leeds.
> Palace, Lowtown (Pudsey).
> Picture House, Maltby.
> Pavilion, Swallownest, near Sheffield.
> Palace Music Hall, Hull.
>
> **November 13th to 15th.**
> Picture Palace, Smallthorne.
> Gaiety Theatre, Wallington (Surrey).
> Globe Cinema, Irlam.

Playdates for a CWS Promotional Film, 1930, printed weekly in the Co-operative News

side of the movement'. As to be expected, CWS productive activities, such as the Middleton Jam Works and the Yarmouth Canning Works were featured. However, a significant development appears to have taken place with the addition of 'several little domestic dramas each with a co-operative moral, together with convincing slogans'.[11] It was obvious that general audiences were unlikely to be responsive to the co-operative ideal if all they were offered were long, detailed examinations of CWS factories, despite the claim of a few years earlier by a co-operative correspondent that to 'show him (the worker) a branch of the CWS activities, with an army of workers engaged in making for use and not for profit, and he is at once impressed'.[12]

The regular screening of domestic story films, advocating co–operation, to general audiences, had become a central activity of CWS film work by January 1928. The use of cinema films advertising the principles of co–operation had been mooted at the 1927 International Co-operative

Alliance Congress held in Stockholm, and the English CWS was quick to follow up the suggestion. In fact, a similar scheme had been attempted in 1921 when the National Joint Committee for Co-operative Capital (NJCCC) declared that through 'pictorial propaganda' the 'gospel of co–operation will be prominently brought before the unconverted'. The proposal required active participation by the local society, who was responsible for exhibition at local cinemas as part of the regular film programme, with special arrangements to advertise the name of the sponsoring society. It was recognised that story films were a necessary element of the scheme as 'the films will be shown to numerous non–co-operators, and, therefore, it is essential that they should not be wearied by too big a dose of co-operation at one sitting'.[13] A series of six films were prepared: *Manufacturing Goods for Use, Not for Making Profit; Marrying Money; Clothing a Statue; The Penny: What Can Be Done With It?; and Economic Power: The Power of Possession*. In the view of a Co-operative News correspondent:

> The project appears to offer a unique method of spreading co-operative principles and advertising local co-operative activities. The committee's enterprise should receive the complete support of the societies in order that the scheme may be carried out in its entirety, and the full advantage obtained from this valuable form of pictorial propaganda.[14]

The scheme was predicated on the involvement of at least 50 societies paying £4 15s per house, per film, per week. Initial costings had proceeded on the assumption that 400 societies would participate. In the event it appears that the minimum number was not achieved and no further reports were forthcoming. It is probable that the 'drama' films screened at the British Empire Exhibition in 1925 hailed back to the 'pictorial propaganda' initiative of 1921.

No doubt weary of the local retail society's enthusiasm to meet the cost of such propaganda, the CWS assumed total financial responsibility for the new scheme of 1928. Distribution was handled by the Co-operative Press Agency, an adjunct to the CWS Publicity Department, who secured exhibition for each film at 1,000 cinemas. The Co-operative News printed regular lists of screenings and venues to ensure the participation of individual co–operators. The first film was *The Magic Basket*, released on 13 February 1928, which was produced for the CWS by Publicity Films Ltd, and lasted 6 minutes.[15] Released to cinemas in the professional 35mm format, 16mm copies were made available to co-operative societies and labour movement organisations for use at branch meetings. The film introduced a style that would serve as the basis of the series for the next five years, namely, brief dramatic sequences, involving the ideal co-operative couple or family, framing the obligatory documentary sequences of CWS production. The flavour is given in a pronouncement for the film provided by a CWS trade journal:

> Glimpses of actual productions will be shown, the finished product in each case being made a component of the contents of the housewife's shopping basket. The audience will have a view of the interior of a co-operative store where the member is withdrawing her dividend. She ultimately finds her way into the drapery department, where a selection of co-operative clothing gives her a new interest in the society of which she is a member.[16]

It is evident that the interest of the potential member was being appealed to through representations of the co-operative experience with which they would be most familiar: popular retail products; a typical Co–op store; fashion; and the dividend. It was hoped that 'non co–operators who see the film, if they are wise people, will follow the example of "Mrs Everett" – they will become loyal purchasing members of a co-operative society, and either save the dividend or put it to the same good use'.[17]

Subsequent titles dealt with individual products and were released as follows: *Bubbles* (soap), released August 1928; *The Cup that Cheers* (tea), released October 1928; *Footsteps* (boots and shoes), released March 1929; *A Matter of Form* (corsets), released August 1929; *What the Diary Told* (soap) released November 1929; *Work and Play* (CWS welfare provision), released January 1930; *The Bright Side of Things* (polish), released January 1930; *Round the Clock* (biscuits), released November 1930; *The King and the Cakes* (flour), released November 1930; *Her Dress Allowance* (drapery), released in both silent and sound versions, December 1930; and *Teaching Him a Lesson* (soap), released in both silent and sound versions, January 1931.[18] Sound films were considered a particularly appropriate medium for 'a democratic organisation like the CWS with principles to propagate as well as commodities to sell'.[19] After March 1931 the CWS discontinued the practice of listing exhibition details in the Co-operative News and precise information about subsequent release dates is hard to determine. Production seems to have been abated for a period; further titles appearing in 1933 with *Back to Back* (men's clothing), and *A Song of the Shirt* (shirts), with *Partners* introducing a less product-oriented approach, with its indication of 'how all members of co-operative societies are partners in a great concern'.[20] *Co-operation in Industry*, and films depicting the Manchester Tobacco Factory Prize Band and the CWS Manchester male-voice choir, were prepared in 1934.

Such was the basic pattern of CWS film activity in the 1930s. Innovations such as colour were readily incorporated, as in *Gallons of Goodness* (1937) which dealt with dairy products, and the Co–op claimed at that time to be 'the only organisation in the country using colour cartoons on the lines of 'Mickey Mouse' for film propaganda'.[21] The first was *The Sweets of Victory* (1937) which lasted five and a half minutes, and promoted 'Lutona' chocolates. Over 6,000 cinema screenings were secured for the film.[22]

Co-op cartoon Sweets of Victory (1937), promoting Lutona chocolates

The screening of CWS films to co-operative and progressive audiences remained a popular and important role for the publicity department. Simultaneous with the cinema campaign of 1928 'societies could have the services of lecturer, operator and all the requirements for an evenings cinema lecture for an inclusive fee of 35s'.[23] The CWS Newcastle Lecture Department declared an excellent response from northern societies in 1930, with bookings for the 1931 season rising to 140, and proving 'a strong stimulus to membership and trade'.[24] It is instructive to contemplate that a parallel scheme was unveiled in the summer of 1929 by the Central Education Committee of the Co-operative Union, which was desirous of utilising film for educational purposes. It entered into agreement with British Film Services Ltd to provide general interest shows at a cost to societies. Despite considerable promotion the scheme appears to have achieved little, probably as it demanded much of the local society, who had to provide accommodation and a minimum guaranteed audience of 500 for each of 20 shows. The comparable CWS show was less demanding and costly, and entirely 'co-operative'.

Accordingly, CWS cinema lectures proved increasingly popular with 237,000 attending 1,196 screenings during the 1937–38 season. The publicity value of the event was carefully thought out and:

> Far from being merely educational gatherings, these lectures were closely allied to the trading activities of the retail societies concerned. Publicity films, coupons, and window displays, together with a systematic visitation of societies by CWS travellers before each event, produced a chain between propaganda and trade which reflected beneficially on sales.[25]

The 1937–38 lectures promoted the products of the CWS Lowestoft Pure Foods factories, and to facilitate that, a new talking film was produced. Over 4,000 specially prepared window displays were made available to participating societies and:

> The problem of inducing audiences to visit the local co-operative stores soon after the lecture was solved by presenting all who attended with a coupon entitling the holder to purchase a box of Waveney Sandwich Cheese or Cheddar Cheese at the reduced price of 3d.[26]

The 1938–39 season was devoted to publicising CWS soap. Two films suitable for that task had been produced in 1937 in *Postman's Knock* and *Merry Monday*.

It was maintained that 'primarily, the modern CWS trade film sets out to entertain, then to instruct, and finally to advertise'.[27] In accordance, films often included musical and comic sequences, sometimes with celebrity performers. A particularly ambitious production was *Co–operette* (1938), shot on the 'new' Dufay colour film stock, a comedy musical featuring Debroy Somers and his band, the dancing of the Co–operettes (six of 'C B Cochran's Young Ladies') and Stanley Holloway recreating his famous character Sam Small, and delivering a monologue on 'T'Co–op'. Released to cinemas in January 1939, the Co-operative News optimistically forecast that it would 'be seen by 5 million people during the first week of its release'.[28]

The CWS Film Library Service was further consolidated in 1938 with the establishment of the CWS National Film Service. The 1936 Co-operative Education Convention of the Co-operative Union had authorised the development of a National Film Service as part of the 'Ten Year Plan for Co-operative Education', wherein 'the importance of the film as a medium for popularising the Co-operative Idea and Ideals was recognised'.[30] Such a task was beyond the Co-operative Union, who approached the CWS for help, and found them sympathetic.

The existing library service, providing a two–hours' programme of CWS publicity films for 35s, was to continue (with no extra charge for screening the show on the afternoon of the same day to members of the Co-operative Women's Guild), with an additional service providing a two–hour purely educational programme with an operator and equipment for between £5 to £6. It was stipulated that at least one CWS advertising film should be included in the programme. A 'well balanced' two–hour display comprised of '1 Travel Talk (two reels), 2 Educational (two reels), 1 Feature (four reels), 1 Comedy (two reels), 1 Cartoon (two reels) and 1 Publicity (one reel)'.[30]

Cheaper rates were available to societies able to supply their own equipment and who were prepared to group together to work on a circuit basis. In addition, under the new service the CWS would produce films for societies and supply equipment and technical advice upon request.

There is little evidence that societies sought out the CWS in the role of film producer, and with the establishment of the Workers' Film Association in 1938, there was much overlapping and duplication of activity.[31] During its first season 300 educational and entertainment films were hired by co-operative societies through the National Film Service as well as 1,620 CWS publicity films.[32] Further progress was achieved during the 1939–40 season, the popularity of which was 'shown by the fact that some 310 educational and entertainment films were hired by Co-operative Societies through the National Film Service and 2,004 CWS publicity films were hired by Co-operative Societies, schools, educational authorities, associations and individuals'.[33] However, war–time conditions eventually forced the 'curtailment of propaganda by Societies'[34], and as a result only 100 educational and entertainment films were hired during the 1940–41 session.

Despite the difficult circumstances brought about by World War II, frustrating the CWS in its aim to provide a comprehensive film service for the movement, some remarkable advances and achievements were possible. Principal amongst those was the establishment of the CWS Film Unit in 1940. Previously the Wholesale Society had relied on the expertise and facilities of the commercial industry, and, the significance of the new situation was percieved by the co-operative press which observed that 'what the CWS has done has been to acquire these same facilities for itself. Personnel from the big London studios and the most modern camera and lighting equipment are now in the service of the Wholesale Society'.[35]

Filming the CWS musical Co-operette, 1938

A fundamental co-operative ideal, itself a crucial motivation for the original establishment of the CWS, was 'universal provision', the complete self-sufficiency of the movement, and total lack of dependency on capitalist industry: 'the CWS has always aimed to manufacture as many as possible of the products they supply to Societies, and through the Societies to co-operators in general; so it was not surprising when the CWS Directors decided that the time had come for them to produce their own films'.[36]

The film unit was under the supervision of George Wynn, a commercial producer whose first contact with CWS publicity films had been in 1931. The unit's first cameraman was Harry Waxman, a technician destined for a celebrated career in the feature film industry.[37] Small professional studio facilities were planned for the film unit in Manchester, and it was claimed 'that no other commercial trading enterprise possesses such up-to-date facilities for making known the value of their own productions'.[38] The first film completed by the unit was a 16 mm sound film of the 1940 Co-operative Congress, held in Glasgow at Whitsuntide. The film unit achieved national prominence with the recording of the Manchester blitz in its film *Manchester Took It Too*, released nationally in the autumn of 1941, and which provided, I understand, the only coverage of a provincial raid. The professionalism of the unit was recognised with contracts fulfilled for the Ministry of Fuel and Power, for which *Boiler House Practice* and *Steam* were produced, and the MOI, for which *Machines and Men* (1942) was produced.

Preparations for celebrating the centenary of the Movement in 1944 had been underway since before the war, with a Planning Committee first meeting in October 1938, and one suggestion that had received much favour was 'the production of a film descriptive of the rise and progress of the Co-operative Movement during the past 100 years'.[39] Furthermore, a film of 'general co-operative interest, starring a well known and popular actress, had been proposed'.[40] No doubt Rochdale's own Gracie Fields was in mind as the ideal candidate, however, the war, and indeed, Gracie's departure to the States with her Italian husband, finally put paid to the more ambitious scheme.

In the event a not immodest project was undertaken by the movement's own film unit in collaboration with producer Sidney Box, the former scenario manager for Publicity Films Ltd. *Men of Rochdale* (1944), 'An intensly human story of the dramatic events surrounding the opening of

Men of Rochdale (1944): Waiting for the Toad Lane Stores to open on the night of 21 December, 1844

Toad Lane and the foundation of the Co-operative Movement' [42], was produced at an impressive cost of £15,000. On the film's release in September 1944, it had been expressed that:

> Many thousands of co-operators will see this film with delight and appreciation, but societies ought not to be satisfied with such audiences. *Men of Rochdale* ought to be seen by audiences of the type that rarely attend co-operative gatherings. It should be seen by trade unionists, shop stewards, socialists, youth groups, service men and women. To them it would be a revelation of the true story which lies behind the local Co-operative Store and the possibilities which are open for the newer pioneers of the 20th Century'.[43]

The inspirational ending to the film certainly accorded with such sentiments and the author would no doubt have been satisfied that by March it had 'reached its 1,000th exhibition in public halls and cinemas throughout England and Wales', also receiving play dates in Canada, New Zealand, Australia, South Africa, the US and Switzerland.[44]

The film, lasting forty-five minutes, recounts, in a fairly theatrical and conventional manner, the establishment of the co-operative store at Toad Lane, Rochdale, in 1844. Despite the hostility of local tradesmen, a particularly notable example being played by John Laurie, the Pioneers are successful, and the film charts the rise of the movement into the twentieth century.

Three other important film projects sponsored by the movement during the war, but which did not involve the CWS film unit, should be mentioned. *Out of the Box* (1942) was commissioned by the Scottish Co-operative Wolesale Society and presented a dramatised story of the eighteenth century Fenwick Weavers, who represented an important antecedent to the establishment of co–operation in Scotland. Remarkably, the film, produced at the Merton Park Studios in London, was shot in both Technicolor (35mm) and black and white (16mm).[46]

The film offers an interesting contrast to *Men of Rochdale*, as it similarly presents an account of the emergence and establishment of co–operation based on the profit–sharing principle of 'dividend'. It is not too cynical to suggest that the Scottish film's release, two years before the Rochdale centenary, was calculated to steal some of the English movement's thunder.

Two Good Fairies (1943) was scripted by the noted philosopher CEM Joad, a popular member of BBC Radio's 'Brains Trust', and was also commissioned by the Scottish Co-operative Wholesale Society. The two good fairies mentioned were the Beveridge Plan and the co-operative movement, and Mr W C Hewitt, a director of the Scottish Society, said the message of the Beveridge Plan was so important that his Society thought it should be given to the people by means of that short film.[35] The film received a good release with distribution to the co-operative movement controlled by the WFA.

Another film representative of the new social consensus that emerged in the war years was *Song of the People* (1945), produced by Maxwell Munden for the CWS. It is probable that the project was realised outside of the movement as the CWS film unit was fully engaged on its first feature, *Men of Rochdale*. The style of the film was considered innovatory and its theme challenging:

> And, with a technique that is entirely new in conception and expression, the story of the people's struggle for liberty during the past two centuries is unfolded in a form never before presented on the silver–screen.
>
> From its opening, *Song of the People* is a film which stirs the imagination, spoken word and music in modern tempo are designed, not only as enjoyable entertainment but also to 'make you think'.[47]

Co-operative critics found it a 'unique film' that chartered:

> The irresistible advance of the common people towards the realisation of their true heritage... There is but one means of ever reaching the heights of universal happiness, and that is by co–operation, by the unselfish collaboration of all in the creation of a truly democratic order of society.[48]

In contrast, the commercial industry found it 'entirely lacking in humour', of possible interest only for 'specialised and leftist' audiences.[49] It comes as no surprise that the trade press should declare it 'propaganda, much of it of a kind that is intolerant of those who honestly differ from many of its points... In spirit and drive it is akin to the sociological subjects formerly put out by the Soviet Union'.[50]

The film was constructed like a pageant, with its narrative charting the irresistable rise of the workers' movement presented in music and song. The Levellers, the Luddites, the Rochdale Pioneers and noted Trade Unionists would have been popular and emotional icons to worker audiences.

Unfortunately, the particular conflation of social, economic, political and cultural factors that created such an inspirational climate for the left, as the nation moved from war to peace, were not replicated again. Despite the fact that the CWS film unit became the production basis on which the labour movement's new National Film Association was predicated, an ambitious programme of ideologically motivated film–making never emerged.[51] Rather the CWS slipped back into its conventional activities of producing films of co-operative interest and providing a general film service to co-operative societies. One important new area of activity was the production of films to aid in the training of co-operative employees. The Joint Committee on Technical Education had made original proposals on the matter in January 1939, stressing that the British movement was falling behind its European partners, and such competitors as the Bacon Marketing Board. Eventually a scheme was agreed that involved the Co-operative Union and the CWS.[52] Evidently, only one 'salesmanship' film was immediately forthcoming with *Behind the Counter* (1941), with preparations obviously having been seriously hampered by the onset of war. The initiative was renewed post–war, and, although hailed as a new film, *Behind the Counter* was reissued, no doubt finding the more stable employment conditions of peace, more conducive to its aims. Milk salesmen and milk sales were the target of a film campaign undertaken in the spring of

1947, which saw the preparation of *Milk Salesmanship* for employees, and *The Milk We Drink* for general audiences. Training films were soon established as part of the CWS film unit's production programme, alongside promotional films and general co-operative subjects, and before long, employees engaged in transport, grocery and food–stuffs, footwear, drapery and outfitting, pharmacy and staff management were benefiting from this new educational technique.

An important new scheme for film distribution in Scotland was commenced by the Scottish Co-operative Wholesale Society in 1948. A specially prepared mobile film unit travelled to remote villages and hamlets, and reported as giving 550 film shows to co-operative and other organisations in its first season.[53]

The CWS inaugurated a similar scheme in September 1950, which was probably a consolidated form of an existing arrangement whereby 'mobile film units' provided several film shows throughout a society's trading area during a given period.[54] The new style displays differed from previous schemes in that they were offered free of charge to co-operative and progressive organisations, as long as they could provide a suitable venue, and ensure an audience of at least 90. Three kinds of show were available: a women's show lasting 75 minutes; a children's show lasting 60 minutes; and a mixed adults show lasting 105 minutes.[55] This type of activity was worrisome to the cinema industry who had long been hostile to the 'free show menace'[56],

Section of crowd viewing CWS films shown by daylight van

The making of the CWS' Woman's Hour film Father Takes the Cake, on the set in the Thames-side studios at Shepperton

traditionally perpetrated by labour groups and religious societies. At the end of World War II that particular paranoia had manifested itself as the '16mm menace', with the cinema trade particularly apprehensive about the release of 16mm projection equipment belonging to various ministries, through disposal boards after the war. Reporting on the issue, as debated at the Manchester and Salford Branch of the Cinematograph Exhibitors' Association, Today's Cinema stressed that 'Particular mention was made of the likelihood of co-operative societies acquiring these sets for the numerous public halls which they controlled'.[57] Therefore, even in the less politically charged atmosphere of the late 1940s, the trade could declare with respect to the new scheme, 'Propaganda for Socialists is the Aim'. The fact that the project involved the screening of feature films, no matter how innocuous their B–movie credentials, continued to make the trade nervous.[58]

It was satisfactorily reported within the movement that 'By the end of July 1951, over 2,059 shows had been given and attendance totalled about 217,000, an average of 105 per show'.[59] On average about 250,000 continued annually to see CWS film shows for the decade. By 1962, 16 roadshow operators were putting on 2,600 shows a year for co-operative societies, 750 of those being exclusively for women. The basic programme format had changed little since the late 1930s and there continued 'A direct link–up with one of the CWS factories' whereby 'examples of their products are given away'.[60] Product films from that period include *Seal of Success* (margarine – 1955), *Father Takes the Cake* (baking ingredients–1957), *Halcyon Days* (paints – c 1961) and *It's in the Can* (canned foods – c1961).

A convenient place to end this survey is with the 1963 CWS centenary celebrations, most visibly marked by the brand new CWS tower which came to dominate the townscape of Manchester. A 30-minute colour film tracing the 100 years history of the CWS was proposed as a suitable replacement for *Men of Rochdale,* the most popular film ever shown by the film section, as a history of the movement'.[61] In the event, the film that was produced, *Symbol of Success*, concentrated largely on the 'co-operative housewife' and her potential democratic participation in the movement. Although of some interest, the film completely lacked the scope and inspiration of its predecessor. A housewife's satisfaction and pride in her ability to attend the quarterly meetings of the CWS, was not the culmination of the 'Co-operative Commonwealth'.

In the two decades that separate the films, the movement had faced important changes in both society and retailing. At least two films had addressed the fundamental problem of declining democratic participation: *Co-operation* (1948); and *It's All Yours* (1954) (produced by a co-operative co-partnership society of film technicians – Documentary Technicians' Alliance Ltd); albeit, in a tentative manner.

At the time of the centenary of its wholesale division the movement was embarking on a programme of rationalisation. The number of independent retail societies was substantially reducing and the status of the professional manager (increasingly drawn from outside the movement) was in the ascendency vis a vis the member. Indicative of those changes, the CWS publicity department was restructured and the film unit disbanded. It exists today in the form of an audio–visual department, largely busied with 'corporate video'.

NOTES

[1] REDFERN, P (1938) The New History of the CWS (London) p197.

[2] See The Wheatsheaf, December 1898, p94. Examples of lantern slides can be found at the CWS library, Manchester.

[3] Box, S (1936) 'Britain's First Advertising Films Were Shown in 1899' in The Commercial Film, March 1936, p6.

[4] Co–operative News, 8 March, 1902, p279.

[5] 'Britain's First Advertising Films Were Shown in 1899', op cit.

[6] Co–operative News, 25 October, 1913, p1421.

[7] Co–operative News, 28 February, 1914, pp 268–269.

[8] Co–operative News, 21 March, 1914, p358. Emphasis added.

[9] For a good general history of the period see : STEVENSON, J. (1984) British Society 1914–45 (London).

[10] See : Pollard, S 'The Foundation of the Co–operative Party', in BRIGGS, A and SAVILLE, J (eds) (1971) Essays in Labour History 1886–1923 (London) and MAGUIRE, P 'Co–operation and Crisis: Government, Co–operation and Politics, 1917–22', in YEO, S. (ed) (1988) New Views on Co–operation (London).

[11] Co–operative News, 23 May, 1925, p3.

[12] Co–operative News, 9 April, 1921, p5.

[13] Co–operative News, 10 September, 1921, p9.

[14] Co–operative News, 9 April, 1921, p5.

[15] A copy of the film is preserved at the North West Film Archive.

[16] The Producer, December, 1927, p32.

[17] Co–operative News, 28 January, 1928, p11.

[18] Some of these films have been preserved at the North West Film Archive.

[19] The Producer, January, 1938, p12.

[20] The Labour Magazine, March, 1933.

[21] Co–operative News, 23 October, 1937, p15.

[22] The Producer, January, 1937, p7.

[23] Co–operative News, 23 November, 1929, p3. The cost was held at 35s until the Second World War and received a generous subsidy from the CWS.

[24] Co–operative News, 10 January, 1931, p11. Other offices were situated at Manchester, London and Bristol.

[25] The Producer, August, 1938, p204.
[26] ibid.
[27] The Producer, January, 1938, pp12–13.
[28] Co–operative News, 21 January, 1939, p1.
[29] CWS National Film Service Catalogue, pI.
[30] CHURCHWARD, F (1938) 'Movement's Screen Debut' in Co–operative Review, November, pp335–336.
[31] For a discussion of the WFA see chapter 2.
[32] Co–operative Union Annual Congress Report, 1939, p80.
[33] ibid. 1940, p76.
[34] ibid. 1941, p63.
[35] Co–operative News, 9 November, 1940, p12.
[36] The Wheatsheaf, January, 1941, p3.
[37] His first feature as cinematographer was *Brighton Rock* (1946).
[38] The Wheatsheaf, op cit.
[39] Co–operative News, 16 September, 1939, p5.
[40] The Co–operative Review, November, 1938, p337.
[41] See BOX, M (1974) Odd Woman Out (London) Ch.12. Box's first full feature after *Men of Rochdale* was *The Seventh Veil* (1945) with James Mason and Ann Todd, Britain's biggest grossing film in the 1940s. Creative personnel Compton Bennett (director) and Reg Wyer (photography) worked on both films.
[42] The Wheatsheaf, June, 1944, pp6–7.
[43] TOPHAM, E (1944) 'Pioneers on the Screen' in the Co–operative Review, October, p151.
[44] Co–operative News, 24 March, 1945, p1.
[45] Today's Cinema, 10 December, 1943, p9.
[46] Co–operative News, 2 May, 1942, p3. Technicolor was an extremely rare and expensive process in wartime Britain. As only 16mm copies have survived, it is difficult to test this claim.
Many films relating to co–operation in Scotland are preserved at the Scottish Film Archive. At the moment the author has no detailed information regarding the use of film by co–operative societies in Scotland.
[47] The Wheatsheaf, May, 1945, pp6–7.
[48] ibid.
[49] Kine Weekly, 17 May, 1945, p23.

[50] ibid.
[51] For further discussion of the National Film Association see chapter 2.
[52] Co–operative Review, January, 1939, p23.; Co–operative News, 25 February, 1939, p14.; Co–operative News, 25 March, 1939, p4.; The Producer, May, 1939, p136.
[53] Mobile Film Units and Cinema Vans had long been a part of the propaganda armoury of both the Left and Right. The Conservative Film Association had first used them in 1925 and Labour groups such as Kino, the WFA and Royal Arsenal Co–operative Society had experimented with them in the 1930s.
[54] For instance a CWS Mobile Film Unit gave nine shows to 1,300 people during a week's visit to the Plymouth area. See Co–operative News, 21 October, 1944, p11.
[55] Co–operative News, 19 August, 1950, p1.; The Producer, September, 1950, p20.
[56] Daily Film Renter, 29 December, 1936, p1.
[57] Today's Cinema, 24 April, 1945, p3.
[58] Today's Cinema, 6 October, 1950, pp3–4.; Today's Cinema, 12 October, 1950, pp3–4. Feature titles included such B–Westerns as *Song of the Range*, *Moon Over Montana*, *The Range Busters* and *Riders of the Dawn*.
[59] Co–operative Review, February, 1952, p37.
[60] The Producer, June, 1962, pp8–9.
[61] ibid.

JOSEPH REEVES: FILMS FOR EDUCATION AND SOCIAL CHANGE

Alderman Joseph Reeves was a towering figure in co-operative education, and the movement's leading proponent of the use of film for educational and cultural purposes. For virtually the whole of the inter-war period (1918-1938) he was the dynamic education secretary of the Royal Arsenal Co-operative Society (RACS), which during that period developed into the second largest co-operative society in Britain.[1] Reeves, although always at the centre of co-operative educational activities, was also a lifelong labour movement activist: an ILP member; a pacifist; the former editor of the Christian Socialist; a Co-operative and Labour Parliamentary candidate for Greenwich; the Secretary-Organiser of the Workers' Film Association (1938-1946); and advisor to the National Film Association (1946-1953).[2] It is within the wider context of socialist activity that Reeves' contributions must be appreciated. Accordingly, John Attfield asserts that Reeves:

> Took part in practically all the major departures in co-operative education and organisation in this period. He was largely the architect of a whole series of new initiatives in RACS educational work: the expansion of classwork in conjunction with the LCC, WEA and other adult education bodies; an exceptionally high standard of cultural activity; the founding of the Woodcraft Folk; overseas travel and the Workers' Travel Association; the pioneering use of film for the working class movement; new forms of co-operative government and the Members' Council.[3]

Reeves was a tireless propagandist in promulgating his views on co-operative education. In stressing that 'state education is to ensure that the individual will function in society according to the point of view of those who control the State. The educational work of the State is to prepare people to be citizens within a capitalist economy',[4] he maintained a fairly traditional position within the socialist dogma. What marked him out was his unrivalled energy and consequent practical application of his ideals, afforded by the resources and structures of the RACS. He saw that his work 'will make bad citizens for capitalism and good citizens for the Commonwealth'.[5] To achieve that, co-operative education must be separate and distinct from State education, although he was never averse to utilising State resources, such as those available to support adult education consequent on the 1918 Education Act, so that 'the workers would be led to see the nature of the society of which they formed a part and would be led to change it'.[6] For Reeves it was co-operative education and not co-operative trade that would transform the acquisitive system into one of mutual aid. The importance of trade was instrumental; it provided the resources necessary for supporting the co-operative education that would bring about social change.

Reeves' theory of co-operative education was essentially experiential. The act of co-operation would teach people as effectively as teaching people co-operation: 'There should be a co-operative purpose in education and an educational purpose in co-operation'.[7] In that sense, the broader cultural activities sponsored by the movement played their part in 'preparing its members for their growing social responsibilities in a society undergoing radical changes'.[8] However, Reeves was careful to maintain that the culture engaged with should have a 'social ethic', and was dismissive of 'concert meetings, bun fights, gala days and fetes', which accounted for the majority of educational funds.[9] In their place he advocated activities 'inspired by the call of a new order based on justice and equality'.[10] He assured his audience that 'there were many authors who had written plays with social change in view, and in running a musical society they should not select militaristic works'.[11] He came to particularly praise the combined endeavours of the five London co-operative societies who staged a massed workers' Pageant at Wembley in 1938, as well as a week's performance of Handel's Belshazzar at the Scala Theatre London, performed by 400 choristers from 15 co-operative choirs and musicians from four London Society orchestras. The latter, with its themes of Jewish captivity, has been adjudicated a 'high point of inter-war musical work of the London Joint Education Committee as regards both the technical quality of the production and the objective of presenting progressive and co-operative ideals through the medium of serious music'.[12]

In 1936 Reeves authored two pamphlets that stand as seminal expressions of his thoughts on education and film: Education for Social Change and The Film and Education.[13] Those documents represent a synthesis of his ideas developed over two decades, and acted as an important stimulus to action within the movement. From the time of his appointment as education secretary of the RACS, Reeves had increasingly come to view modern publicity techniques as an integral support to educational progress. Chief amongst them were modern mass communications, of which film had a unique contribution to make. As early as 1921, in suggestions on 'How To Reach The People', Reeves was advising that 'Systematic propaganda and scientific advertising might contribute more to the realisation of the Co-operative Commonwealth than any combination of circumstances one could imagine.' He advocated:

> Appeal to people through all legitimate agencies to see the value of co-operation - through the capitalist press, by posters and showcards, by electric sign and tram ticket, by suggestion and by direct appeal, by press notices and by the printers. He would have the co-operative message on the breakfast table with the morning paper; he would have it on the cinematograph screen.[14]

Accordingly, Reeves was instrumental in introducing the film medium in support of the RACS educational programme. Commencing in 1922, film shows were given 'to children for the purpose of counter-acting the effect of the sensational film'.[15] With the opening of the Tooting Co-operative Hall in 1925, a cinematograph license was sought and granted, and regular shows were presented, with, for a time in 1929, the Hall becoming home to the London Workers' Film Society.[16] Following the introduction of sound, exhibition once again reverted to portable apparatus for reasons of cost. The silent Soviet classic, Eisenstein's *The General Line* (1929), which extolled the virtues of collectivised farms, was purchased for £30, and screened on over 100 occasions.

RACS Mobile Film Unit, 1938

A film illustrating the society's activities had been prepared in 1921, which included views of the Brixton bakery, the society farm, 'Shornells' and the society education centre, and a football match between employee clubs.[17] Twelve years elapsed before the venture was repeated, with a film 'taken of Children's Day at the Crystal Palace on the occasion of the International Congress'.[18] *Workers Education* (1937) was a sound film depicting the society's educational work, and *People With a Purpose* (1939), was made, at a cost of £1,200, to celebrate the education department's 60th birthday. Film shows for members were a regular feature of the education programme, with over 100 exhibitions arranged for the 1938 season. To cope with the demand the society invested in a mobile film unit, probably the first independent society to do so. The capability of the vehicle was detailed in The Producer:

> The mobile film unit will convey films (stored in specially designed racks), sound equipment (projector, transformer, microphone, gramophone turntable, etc), and screen, to the various halls at which shows will be given. The floor of the van has been specially insulated to prevent vibration, and a platform made on top for use by the cameraman. The body of the van is finished red and cream, the society standard colour scheme.[19]

In 1938 Reeves declared that:

> With the invention of the 16mm non-flam film, I was convinced that the time had come for the workers' movements to work out ways and means whereby the film could be used to make known our social aims, and for the purpose of counter-acting the subtle propaganda for the existing order of society which comes to us from Hollywood and elsewhere.[20]

The film work undertaken at RACS was appreciated as a limited contribution to that aim. However, it was characteristic of Reeves that he sought to achieve more. Acutely aware of the shortage of suitable films, he 'came to the conclusion that the only solution of the problem was for the workers' movements to enter into the field of film production'.[21] As an executive member of the National Association of Co-operative Education Committees (NACEC), he supported the establishment of a film section to augment the educational and propaganda work of the Association, and to which Reeves was not surprisingly appointed Secretary in 1936. From this position he urged that education committees should provide the lead in the use of film for educational purposes. It was that action which essentially placed him at variance with the emerging film plans of the Co-operative Union and CWS, which crystallised in the CWS National Film Service in 1938. The NACEC had been founded in response to the lack of representation granted to education committees on the Co-operative Union structures, and Reeves was sceptical of the Union's appreciation of film as a medium for co-operative education as he understood it. In their alliance with the CWS, he could only consider the Co-operative Union's action as a further consolidation of the interest of trade. In fact the Co-operative Union had declined an invitation to appoint a representative to the Film Committee, and pursued their own line of enquiry with regard to providing educational films as specified under the Ten Year Plan for Co-operative Education. The differences of opinion created some friction, and the general arguments were regularly paraded in the co-operative press.[22]

Reeves first outlined his scheme for co-operative film education at the NACEC Conference held at Swanwick, Derbyshire, in September 1936. It was that address which formed the basis of the report 'The Film and Education'. He called for the formation of a 'National Co-operative Film Society'(NCFS), of which, participating societies would be shareholders, pledged to the regular exhibition of films provided by the NCFS.[23] Response was satisfactory, such that the NACEC established a film department in June 1937, with nearly 20 societies installing projection equipment on its advice. Alternatively, the film department offered to provide a full road show service with films, operator and projector, and within six months 700 such programmes were given.[24] For efficiency, societies were encouraged to form 'circuits', 'so that each society with a projector is provided with a new programme of films every week during the winter months'.[25] Film programmes were compiled from the libraries of Gaumont British and the Communist Party supported Kino Films Ltd, providing an idiosyncratic mix of nature-study films (of the Mary Field variety), classic 1930s documentaries, worthy epics such as *Jew Suss* (1934), progressive European masterpieces like *Kameradschaft* (1931) and socialist newsreels and propaganda, such as *News from Spain* and *War is Hell*.[26] Reeves, in particular, appreciated the importance of combining entertainment with education and propaganda, a strategy he had been faithful to since the Saturday morning film shows for members' children had commenced in the early 1920s.

Reeves' visions extended beyond the co-operative movement, and he envisaged a film organisation that embraced the full labour movement. The NACEC was not a body capable of engaging in large scale film production, and it was becoming apparent that the CWS, the one existing body capable of such a contribution, would remain in alliance with the Co-operative Union, and effectively out of the reckoning.[27] Reeves found the sympathetic attitude he was seeking at the Joint Film Committee (JFC) of the TUC and Labour Party, which had been formed in 1936 for the purpose of promoting film within those two democratic organisations.[28] Obviously impressed by the initiative of the film department of the NACEC, the JFC invited Reeves' participation 'To prevent overlapping and duplication'.[29] An ironic outcome in view of the lack of co-operation between the NACEC and the CU/CWS. A report issued in March 1938 proposed the formation of a Labour Film Service, clearly modelled on the film department of the NACEC. Reeves' dreams were realised in the Summer of 1938 with the establishment of the Workers' Film Association (WFA), the body, he hoped, that would be responsible for the film service for the entire labour movement. Its first appointment was Alderman Joseph Reeves as Secretary-Organiser, necessitating his resignation as education secretary to the RACS, but with him remaining secretary to the film department of the NACEC until March 1940, when it was agreed such a function was no longer necessary.[30] The co-operative movement's involvement with the new body remained problematic. Discussions with regard to the Co-operative Union's and CWS's actual participation were periodically reported throughout the early years of the war, yet the CWS in particular remained intransigent. In April 1942, it was agreed that the NACEC should become a full member of the WFA and they were joined by the Scottish Co-operative Wholesale Society later in the year.[31] That same year the WFA reached agreement whereby the CWS film unit would undertake production for the Association, with the Education Executive of the Co-operative Union attaining representation on the National Joint Film Committee of the WFA, providing at least a nominal recognition by the co-operative movement.

Not surprisingly, the initial work of the Association resembled that developed by the film department of the NACEC, with the distribution and exhibition of educational and propaganda films being the main activity. As we have seen, Reeves' desire was to see the direct production of films by labour groups, and his ambitions were apparent in one of his first pronouncements for the WFA:

> I would like to see railway unions providing a film on the life of a railway man, the Transport Workers' Union one on the risks a motor driver takes from day-to-day providing transport for the people and goods, indeed the life of the great army of workers, builders, miners, seamen, printers, electricians and others should be dramatised because their lives and work are the stuff of which life is made.[32]

Reeves had been instrumental in realising the London Joint Education Committee's 'Five Year Film Plan' which commenced with *Advance Democracy* (1938), and dramatised the political awakening of a London dock worker, with the help of his wife, an active Co-op guildswoman.[33] Therefore, the Association expended much effort to influence the production of workers' films.[34] Due to the war, only a handful of films were made, notably *The Builders* (1939), for the Amalgamated Union of Building Trade Workers, *Unity is Strength* (nd) for the Amalgamated Engineering Union, and *The Republic of Children* (1939) for the Woodcraft Folk.

In the restrictive environment of war, film hire and display became the prime activities of the Association, and, even here, provision was made more difficult due to the general lack of equipment and parts.[35] However, film displays did increase substantially, to an estimated 15,000 attained in 1944. Demand was undoubtedly stimulated 'on account of the exclusive distribution rights of the great proportion of Russian films released for showing on sub-standard stock', granted to the WFA, who was also distributing on behalf of the Polish, Czechoslovakian and Chinese Governments.[36] The purchase of a Wolseley car, immediately fitted as a mobile film unit in 1943, substantially added to the service. 'Schemes for showing films at Emergency Evacuation Centres, in air-raid shelters and in reception areas' were a particularly attractive departure, giving access, in an incomparable manner, to the general public for the Association's propaganda.[37]

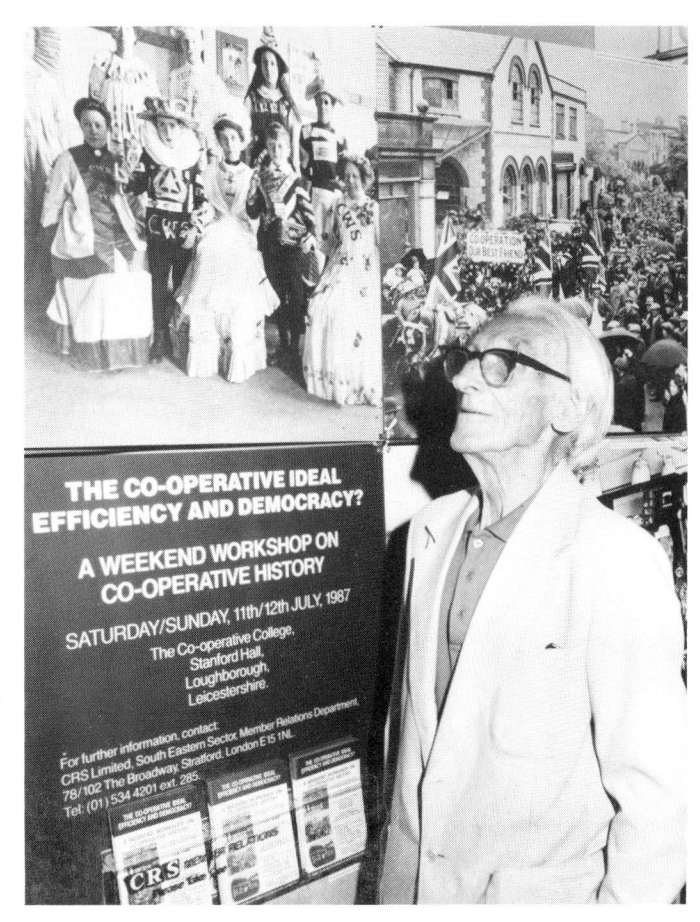

Ralph Bond, director of Advance Democracy (1938), at the Co-op History Weekend, Stanford Hall, 1987

With the resources and networks accorded by the WFA, Reeves was in a position to realise a long cherished dream, a synthesis of his twin passions of education and film. Early in 1939 he had advocated that:

> Film Societies for showing and producing films should be formed for the purpose of propagating the principles of socialism, co-operation, and trade unionism. Summer and weekend schools to discuss film production should be organised. If this is done, gradually we shall find the Workers' Movement becoming film-minded.[38]

Film schools, usually a weekend, sometimes week-long, were regularly sponsored by the WFA, and always attracted high profile lecturers such as Thorold Dickinson, Michael Balcon, Basil Wright, George Elvin, Paul Rotha, Sidney Bernstein, Roy Boulting, Bernard Miles, Edgar Anstey, Arthur Elton, Dilys Powell, Basil Dearden, Mary Field and of course Joseph Reeves.[39] The schools combined lectures, discussions and screenings, with practical demonstrations, in an effort to improve the film appreciation of the workers, and their practical knowledge of film production. Such endeavours would find further expression in the post-war film society movement, in which the co-operative movement was active, sponsoring such groups as the Slough Co-operative Film Society, the Dagenham Co-operative Film Society and the Birkenhead Co-operative Film Society.

The WFA was in a buoyant mood by the time victory was declared in the summer of 1945. Its energies were devoted to the establishment of a majority Labour Government and 'During the general election loud speaker equipment to the value of £10,000 was sold to local Labour Parties, which added considerably to the efficiency of their electioneering campaign'.[40] Reeves himself was elected MP for Greenwich at the July election. As a consequence the Association underwent considerable transformation, emerging as a new body, the National Film Association, in November 1946. For many months 'the WFA had been negotiating with the CWS and Co-operative Union, with a view to the establishment of a central film organisation for the whole political Labour, trade union and co-operative movements'.[41] At long last a Film Association, fully representative of the entire labour movement, was in being. No longer in 'opposition', the labour movement's film service could claim itself as 'national', and sought 'To encourage and promote within all sections of the democratic, labour, and co-

WFA Film School, Beatrice Webb House, 1950

operative movements the use of the film as a medium of democratic education, information, propaganda, and social enlightenment'.[42]

Joseph Reeves was retained as Advisor to the NFA until it was disbanded in 1953, by which time the Conservatives were back in power. It achieved relatively little, largely continuing with a predictable programme of film shows and film schools, with the single innovation of publishing a bi-monthly journal, which after a short while became a quarterly. The new Association was totally reliant on the CWS Film Department, and its activities extended little beyond those of the CWS National Film Service. Film production was particularly disappointing, with the Labour Government commissioning only one title in *Their Great Adventure* (1947).[43]

Between the 1930s and 1950s political culture in Britain radically transformed. The labour movement became more placid, and its more limited vision was evident in the disbandment of the NFA whose object had been 'to stimulate the use of films by the democratic movements', with the surprising claim that 'this objective has been achieved'.[44] The quiescent complacency inherent in the regular screening of film shows to progressive audiences was a far cry from Reeves' belief in the workers' appropriation of the technology of cinema, and the potential of film for education and social change:

> A new hope will come to those entrusted with the task of making known the way to the new world, because its new appeal will go direct to the hearts and minds of people accustomed to be moved by the technique of the 'movie'.[45]

NOTES

[1] For an excellent history of education at the RACS see ATTFIELD, J (1981) With Light of Knowledge (London).

[2] ibid. p41.; Co–operative News, 2 November, 1935, p1.
With respect to the Co–operative Movement, it has been claimed that 'He holds what is probably a record for service on education committees, national and sectional, totalling 20'. See Co–operative News, 3 September, 1938, p1.

[3] With Light of Knowledge, op cit p42.

[4] Co–operative News, 12 December, 1931, p5.

[5] ibid.

[6] REEVES, J (1944) A Century of Rochdale Co–operation (London) p45.

[7] Co–operative News, 12 December, 1931, p5.

[8] A Century of Rochdale Co–operation, op cit p46.

[9] Quoted in ATTFIELD, J., op cit p43.

[10] A Century of Rochdale Co–operation, op cit p97.

[11] Co–operative News, 12 December, 1931, p5.

[12] With Light of Knowledge, op cit p48.

[13] REEVES, J (1936) Education For Social Change (Manchester); REEVES, J (1936) The Film and Education (Stoke–on–Trent).

[14] Co–operative News, 5 November, 1921, p10.

[15] The Film and Education, op cit p6.

[16] HOGENKAMP, B (1986) Deadly Parallels (London) p37.

[17] Co–operative News, 5 November, 1921, p10.

[18] The Film and Education, op cit p8. Some of the RACS films are preserved at the ETV archive.

[19] The Producer, November, 1938, p301.

[20] Co–operative News, September 1938, p7.

[21] ibid.

[22] The Co–operative Union's case is argued in : Co–operative News, 14 May, 1938, p2. The NACEC case is argued in : Co–operative News, 21 May, 1938, p3.

[23] Full details of the scheme are presented in The Film and Education, op cit pp16–19.

[24] Co–operative Youth, May, 1938, pp118–119.

[25] REEVES, J (1938) Co–operator's Yearbook, pp67–69.
[26] ibid.
[27] In fact by early 1938 the CWS was refusing to permit the circulation of its publicity films through the Film Department of the NACEC. See Co–operative News, 26 February, 1938, p3.
[28] Two excellent histories of the labour movement and film in the inter–war period can be consulted.
JONES, SG (1987) The British Labour Movement and Film, 1918–39, (London) and HOGENKAMP, B., op cit
[29] Quoted in JONES, S.G., op cit p153.
[30] The services of Reeves were 'lost' between the autumn of 1939 and summer of 1941, when he acted as advisor to the MOI.Film Division. It is apparent that his particular talents were not appreciated, so he left. That, in combination with the war in general, accounts for the 'slow' progress of the WFA in the early war years. See Co–operative Review, December 1939, p419.; Co–operative News, 28 June, 1941, p8.
[31] Co–operative News, 11 April, 1942, p5.; A Century of Rochdale Co–operation, op cit p99.; WFA Annual Report 1942, p4.
[32] REEVES, J (1939) 'Films and Propaganda' in Co–operative Youth, February, pp72–74.
[33] For further details see Chapter 3.
[34] See for instance the first catalogue issued by the WFA in 1939, pp4–5.
[35] To maintain its roadshow service, projection equipment was borrowed from the South Suburban Co–operative Society, TUC, Labour Party branches and individuals. See WFA Annual Report, 1943, p2.
[36] Co–operative News, 19 December, 1942, p15.
[37] Kine Weekly, 9 January, 1941, p4.
[38] Films and Propaganda, op cit p74.
[39] Programmes of WFA Film Schools are filed at the TUC library.
[40] WFA Catalogue, 1945, p1.
[41] Co–operative News, 19 January, 1946, p1.
[42] Co–operative News, 5 October, 1946, p16.
[43] The film remains unseen by scholars. However plans are underway to make it available for the 1994 Festival of Films on Co–operation.
[44] Film User, September 1953, p476.
[45] Films and Propaganda, op cit p74.

FHW COX: FILMS FOR PROPAGANDA AND POLITICAL CHANGE

This chapter will concentrate on co-operative film-making in the politically charged period of the 'People's Front', and the early years of World War II. Passionate elements on the Left confronted the combined evils of fascism and a National Government determined on appeasement. The British co-operative movement had watched with dismay as the liberties of co-operators had been challenged, and national co-operative movements had been threatened, by fascist dictatorships. 'Unity' became the progressives' aim, and 'Peace, Freedom and Democracy' their battle cry. In a letter to the Co-operative News, Joseph Reeves, the prospective Labour and Co-operative Parliamentary Candidate for Greenwich, and who in 1937 would be the main driving force in the production of the movement's key 'Popular Front' film, *Advance Democracy*, called for service to the cause of world peace and social justice, and demanded 'a conference of all the elements opposed to this reactionary Government for the purpose of preparing a 'People's Front' programme'. [1] In the event, the Parliamentary Labour Party resisted calls for alliance with the Independent Labour Party, Communist Party and the Socialist League et al, from which it had consistently taken abuse during the decade, and many branches of the Co-operative Party, not wishing to jeopardise their relationship with the Labour Party, were similarly inclined.

However, action for unity within the co-operative movement did take place. The 1930s was strewn with causes for the passionate socialist and co-operator. The activist marched in demonstrations against Fascism and War, and for Republican Spain. Hospitality was given to hunger marchers, unemployment was campaigned against, and camps were established to provide for the Basque children evacuated from Bilbao. [2] Films played their part in raising awareness about such issues, and, with respect to the Spanish Civil War, the contribution made by sympathizers within the established film industry, such as Thorold Dickinson, Sidney Cole and Ivor Montagu, is well documented. [3]

A particular centre of activity within the co-operative movement was the film unit of the London Co-operative Society Political Committee, under the supervision of F H W Cox. London Co-operative Society was the largest society in the world and thus had considerable resources available to support propaganda activities. The society's political committee was an important body in the London labour movement, with influential members like Alfred Barnes MP, Chairman of the Co-operative Party. Cox had come to the attention of the Political Committee with his 'amateur' films of London Co-operative Society International Co-operative Day fetes, beginning in 1932. He had a wide appreciation of the value of film to the co-operative movement and appealed for the formation of a National Co-operative Film Society at the Brighton Co-operative Union Education Convention of 1936. His ideas were subsequently circularised in the widely read co-operative journal, The Millgate, and relate closely to those discussions taking place within the National Association of Co-operative Education Officials (NACEC), that led to its formation of a film department in the same period. [4]

Cox felt that 'the weapons of progress and propaganda in the hands of our opponents are far superior to anything we possess', and he berated the lack of preparation by the movement and warned that 'Until we stop being fifty years behind the times and until we take advantage of radio, press, and films to the fullest extent of which we are able we shall remain at the mercy of capitalism'. [5] He conformed to the conventional view point on the Left that saw the mass media as a soporific, helping to keep the masses satisfied with their lot in life [6], and angry that 'we are content to leave this weapon almost entirely in the hands of our enemies'. [7] Cox's response was a call to action to co-operators, suggesting co-ordinated activity by societies, grouped in a National Co-operative Film Society. The basis of the plan, and his original contribution to the debate, was the establishment of a film unit to supply the films, utilising the cheaper 16 mm sound film. He considered that 'A very modest outlay would suffice to fit up and equip a

A battery of cameramen who filmed the Wembley Pageant.

studio for the production and processing of films', and even proposed a scheme to finance the venture, calculating that:

> One-tenth of a penny in the pound of sales would provide more than sufficient money for such a studio equipped with cameras, lights and scenery for indoor sets, a laboratory for processing, and work rooms for the editing and production of films, including the payment of the necessary salaries. [8]

It is instructive to note that Cox's ideal was for self-sufficiency, proclaiming 'that we should strike out into this new field on our own initiative and resources so that, instead of trailing behind, we shall for once be in the van of progress'. [9] Cox's arguments received endorsement from S E L Moir, Director of the London University Film Society, and President of the Sub-Standard (16 mm) Film Society, who, not surprisingly, was particularly supportive of the advantages claimed for 16 mm film production:

The natural and rapid development at this stage would show the need for an adequate production studio, working solely on 16 mm, and equipped for sound. The satisfactory planning of this would necessitate the calling together of those who understand both the aims of our movement and the particular technique of 16 mm film. [10]

The general debate and manoeuvrings engaged in by the Co-operative Union, CWS and NACEC in the period 1936-40, did not lead to the establishment of a co-operative film studio or film unit representative of the whole movement, along the lines argued by Cox and Moir. In the event film-making activity, with a particularly political motivation, was developed by Cox under the auspices of the London Co-operative Society Political Committee. The three-man 'film department' established by Cox, was in accordance with the ideas he had previously promoted, and claimed to pioneer recording sound direct on 16mm film. For reasons of cost and efficiency, Cox had championed the production of films on the sub-standard format. He considered the original production on 35 mm, with subsequent reduction to 16 mm, needlessly wasteful. However, his approach had led to serious technical difficulties, as the available 16 mm sound technology did not allow for the subsequent editing of the exposed film. Cox later summed up the initial difficulties faced by the embryonic film department, and the subsequent action that was taken in the best co-operative tradition: 'we not only had to master these processes, but also to produce the apparatus to enable us to carry them out in the size of film which we were determined to use'. [11]

The film department of the London Co-operative Society Political Committee was established in September 1937 with a grant of £1,500, with a remit to produce 3 films: a news-reel, a documentary and a feature. To take up the assignment, Frank Cox, an 'employee of a big wireless firm and expert in sound recording', resigned his job. [12] The first two films were completed in collaboration with the production company, Pelly and Healey, and considered the 'first fruits of early experiments in the science of direct sound recording'. [13] *Peace Parade* (1937) was a news-reel of the London Co-operative Society's Hyde Park peace demonstration, and *People Who Count* (1937) a portrait of London Co-operative Society, with a commentary by Co-operative MP, and former cabinet minister, A V Alexander. [14]

The final production of the programme appears to have been the sole work of the unit, and involved the adaptation of 'the most nearly professional 16mm camera', the Kodak Special. With that a twenty-minute 'feature' film, *?Utopia* (1938), was produced. Its success directly stimulated several leading equipment manufacturers to experiment with the technology. [15] The film, a satire on conditions in home and industry in contemporary England, was described by the Daily Worker as an 'entertaining skit upon the Tory point of view about slums, rehousing, malnutrition and rearmament, and gives the irrefutable Socialist answer'. [16]

The unit achieved prominence within the movement with an ambitious project released as *Towards Tomorrow* (1938). On 2 July 1938, Co-operative Day, a massed pageant, involving 3,000 artists, and enjoyed by an audience of 60,000 in the Empire Stadium, was presented as the 'Wembley Festival of Co-operation'. It had been sponsored by the London, South Suburban and Watford societies at a cost of £15,000, with a scenario by

Montague Slater, production by André van Gyseghem, and music by Alan Bush. The day long programme included clowns, community singing and a massed Woodcraft Folk tent pitching display, whilst the inequities and injustices of capitalism, represented 'by effigies of Wealth with a bodyguard of thugs armed with whips', followed by the inevitable rise of the workers' movement, were paraded before an enthusiastic audience. The event stands as a high-spot of inter-war 'culture and commitment'. Cox had arranged for 'A film squad of 14, comprising seven cameramen, sound recorders and electricians, [to shoot] a colour film of the *Wembley Pageant*'. Three cameras were actually on the Stadium roof. A number were on the arena itself, and one spent a lone vigil underneath the centre stage. [18]

The fifty-minute colour film was considered a 'triumph of the pioneering efforts of Mr Cox in his experiments to popularise the 16 mm directly-recorded film'. [19] The film had cost less than £500, and Cox maintained that to have commissioned it from the commercial industry would have cost in excess of £5,000. [20] *Towards Tomorrow* found widespread distribution amongst co-operative societies and even further afield, with copies acquired by the Central Union of Distributive Societies of Finland, the Midland Co-operative Wholesale of Minneapolis, Minnesota, the Canadian Wheat Pool of Saskatchewan and the Eastern Co-operative League of New York. [21]

FHW Cox (right) being congratulated on his Pageant Film (1938)

Shooting of The New Recruit (1939) at the Gaumont Studios

Other films were turned out in fairly rapid succession, and represented a mix of factual and fiction subjects: *The Awakening of Mr Cole* (1938), the story of a modern day Scrooge: *Fashion Parade* (1938), publicising the society's fashion department; *Each for All* (c1938), descriptive of the socialist state within the beehive; *Potter's Clay* (1939), showing the child as clay in the hands of its teachers and parents; and *A New Recruit* (1939), a propagandist feature film with the Conservative Party in the role of villain.

With the onset of War in September 1939, the film department immediately set about adapting to the new conditions, its first wartime release being *The Rape of Czecho-Slovakia* (1939). This was a 'found' documentary, utilising existing film footage, and the status of the London Co-operative Society Political Committee film department was evident in the participation of Basil Wright, who provided, and spoke, the commentary. [22] Cox produced, and Jiri Weiss, former documentary director of A-B Films, Prague, directed the twenty minutes film. [23] Czecho-Slovakian political exiles, Dr Benes and M. Jan Masaryk declared the film 'an epic feature, glorifying democracy and national independence'. [24] The film clearly accorded with the mood of the time, and achieved a limited general release, where it seems it was well received. It appears probable that *The Rape of Czecho-Slovakia* was 'the first co-operative film to be shown in public picture houses on the same basis as other documentaries'. [25]

The profile of the unit was high, and in March 1940 it was announced that J B Priestley would be preparing a script and commentary for a film, to be made by the recently renamed 'Pioneer Films', titled Britain Re-born. I have no evidence that the project got further than the proposal stage. However, the incident is illustrative of the high-regard with which the unit was held. Despite major set-backs, which included the loss of two staff members killed on ARP duty, and bomb damage to the studio in Gray's Inn Road, twice hit by enemy action, Pioneer Films made remarkable progress, providing a creditable 'alternative' to the documentaries of the MOI supplied by the Crown Film Unit.

At a time when British propaganda could barely mount a coherent strategy on the current crisis, Pioneer Films had a strong message to promote, and controversially held up for discussion the type of post-war world for which Britain was fighting. [27] By December 1941 seven films had been produced, two of them in colour. A particularly interesting film, of which unfortunately a copy does not appear to have survived, was *The Home Front* (1940). The twenty-minute film offered a radically different view of war-time Britain than the officially sponsored documentaries such as *The First Days* (1939), *The Front Line* (1940) and *Britain Can Take It* (1940), with their cheery cockneys and stoical humour. In contrast, *Home Front* depicted 'shopkeepers doing a little profiteering on the quiet; rich women shoppers doing a bit of private food hoarding during the early days of the War'. The moral of the film was 'a square deal and a square meal for everyone'. [28] Typically the film looked forward to a fair Peace when, given the interpretation of a Co-operative News reporter, 'we must demand - and secure! - a life worth living for everybody. No black out in the streets and no black out in human life. Real democracy is the end to strive for'. [29]

Other titles concentrated their attack on fascism, beginning with *It Must Not Happen Here* (1940), which showed 'how the German people have suffered under the nazi regime, and how democratic institutions are trampled underfoot as the freedom of the people is destroyed'. [30] It was followed by *Mr Smith Wakes Up* (1940), a film depicting the political awakening of the ordinary man. [31] The films were all given a trade show, and presumably attained some measure of distribution. For instance *Mr Smith Wakes Up* was considered by one observer as one of 'the co-operative movement's greatest efforts so far to bring democratic film propaganda before the general public'. [32] It is somewhat surprising that radical propaganda of that kind could receive wide dissemination, especially in view of the difficulties faced by organs of the radical and progressive press, such as the Daily Worker and the Daily Mirror. [33]

After 1941, reports on the unit's activities dried up, and it is acceptable to speculate that somehow its film-making was being proscribed through such available measures as the call-up of key personnel or rationing of necessary material. As the movement did not declare a conspiracy, it is possible that general conditions, and the loss of personnel and material through enemy action, inevitably brought about a curtailment of activity. Either way, only one further project was reported, and, indicative of the situation, was 18 months in the making. A colour film telling the story of the Chinese Industrial Co-operatives was commenced in the Autumn of 1943, and only completed in the spring of 1945. Released as *Gung Ho*, which apparently translates as 'Work Together', the twenty-five-minute film, made with the assistance of the Anglo-Chinese Development Agency, had Edgar Snow re-enacting his original role in the saga. [34]

This examination of the movement's film-making response to the rise of fascism would be incomplete without a consideration of the 'Five Year Plan of Film Propaganda' undertaken by the London Joint Education Committee. In November 1937, the four big metropolitan societies - London, Royal Arsenal, South Suburban and Enfield Highway - announced their intention to spend £1,000 a year on the production of a twenty minutes film. [35] The driving force behind the plan was Joseph Reeves, who ensured that production would be on 35mm, and who provided a draft scenario for the first film, which sought 'to illustrate the struggles of the workers to achieve social and economic freedom'. [36]

Advance Democracy was released in October 1938, and stands as the prime example of the 'Popular Front' film produced in Britain with its call for 'united action on the part of all men of goodwill against the menace of fascism'. [37] It was directed for the Realist Film Unit by a communist, Ralph Bond, arguably the key figure in the inter-war workers' cinema; it had workers' songs arranged by Benjamin Britten and sung by the Norbury Co-operative Choir; it featured two players from Unity Theatre; and had an address by Co-operative MP, A V Alexander. The film was a conscious attempt to achieve realism, and the very 'ordinariness' of the central couple, marvellously captured by Bond, stands in stark contrast to the theatricality, and wavering northern accents, of *Men of Rochdale*. The film proclaimed the watch words of the Popular Front: 'Peace, Freedom and Democracy', and it was maintained that 'the film could not appear at a more apposite moment; it may articulate for many the emotions they have not yet learnt to analyse and control'. [38] The end sequence in particular was a stirring example of the active commitment and enthusiasm of thousands of workers as they marched in the traditional May Day parade across London, the sequence enlivened by a musical montage consisting of the Internationale, Keep The Red Flag Flying and other labour songs. The continued involvement of leading British composers with workers' music groups was recorded by co-operative film-makers, with Michael Tippett being captured at a RACS school. The next, and final, film produced under the scheme was *Voice of the People* (1939), 'which expressed in pictorial form the struggles of the workers to obtain their present important place in the state'. [39] The film was again produced by the Realist Film Unit, with Bond this time producing, and Lennox Berkely conducting the music.

The 'Five Year Film Plan', came to a halt with the commencement of hostilities. Taken in conjunction, the initiatives of Frank Cox at the London Co-operative Society Political Committee, the London Joint Education Committee, and Royal Arsenal Co-operative Society, which, as we have seen, had sponsored *People With a Purpose* in 1939, represent a significant investment in film-making by aspects of the co-operative movement on the eve of the war. The continuation of propaganda film-making by Cox in the early war years, and the progress of Joseph Reeves at the Workers' Film Association have received little attention by film historians. However those film-makers, and other activists on the Left, have left an example of political film-making of which co-operators and socialists should ever be proud.

NOTES

[1] Co-operative News, 5 September, 1936, p3.

[2] NEWENS, S. (1988) Working Together. A Short History of the London Co-operative Society Political Committee (London). For a view of the Left in the 1930s see KLUGMANN, J 'Introduction: The Crisis in the Thirties : A View from the Left' in CLARK, J, HEINEMANN, M, MARGOLIES, D, SNEE, C (eds) (1970) Culture and Crisis in Britain in the 30s (London).

[3] See DICKINSON, T (1984) 'Experiences in the Spanish Civil War', Historical Journal of Film, Radio and TV, 4; COLE, S. (1938) 'Shooting in Spain', Cine-Technician, 4. The Co-operative Union's 'Milk for Spain' campaign was the movement's principal response to the crisis. To maximise support the Film Department of the NACEC distributed four films for use at demonstrations: *Spanish Earth* (1937); *News from Spain* (1937); *Madrid Today* (1937); and *The Basque Children* (nd). See Co-operative News, 27 November, 1937, p2 and p9.

[4] COX, FHW (1936) 'A National Co-operative Film Society', The Millgate, October, pp39–40.

[5] ibid p39.

[6] Much of the writing on cinema, emanating from the Left, is collected in MACPHERSON, D (ed) (1980) Traditions of Independence (London).

[7] 'A National Co-operative Film Society', op cit p40.

[8] ibid.

[9] ibid. This was essentially a challenge to the CWS, who at that time were reliant on capitalist producers for their publicity films. As we have seen, they became self–sufficient in 1940.

[10] MOIR, SEL (1937) 'Co-operative Films – When?', The Millgate, January, pp200–201. In this article the author makes reference to the 'unofficial' Co-operative Film Council. I have found no further references to this body.

[11] Co-operative News, 5 November, 1938, p8.

[12] Co-operative News, 27 May, 1939, p7.

[13] ibid.

[14] A copy of 'Peace Parade', thought 'lost', was recently acquired by the Imperial War Museum. A copy of 'People Who Count' is preserved at the National Film Archive.

[15] Co-operative News, 10 September, 1938, p3. A patent was soon applied for by the film department who had 'visions of this idea being patented by a

commercial firm and ourselves being made to pay for its use'. See Co-operative News, 28 January, 1939, p2.

[16] Quoted in HOGENKAMP, B (1986) Deadly Parallels (London). p184–185.

[17] Co-operative News (Special Supplement), 9 July, 1938; The Producer, August 1938, pp201–202.

[18] Co-operative News (Special Supplement), 9 July, 1938.

[19] Co-operative News, 17 September, 1938, p5.

[20] The Producer, October, 1938, p264.

[21] Co-operative News, 17 December, 1939, p3.

[22] Wright was a leading member of the Documentary Film Movement, directing films for both the Empire Marketing Board and GPO, before establishing his own unit, Realist Films, in 1937.

[23] Co-operative News, 14 October, 1939, p3.

[24] Co-operative News, 23 December, 1939, p6.

[25] Co-operative Review, February 1940, p78. Described as 'A Film All Co-operators Should See', exhibition dates were given in the Co-op press. See Co-operative News, 20 January, 1940, p1; Co-operative News, 3 Feb, 1940, p15; Co-operative News, 9 March, 1940, p9.

[26] Co-operative News, 8 March, 1940, p12.

[27] For a discussion of British propaganda in World War Two see MCLAINE, I (1979) Ministry of Morale (London).

[28] Co-operative News, 9 March, 1940, p4.

[29] ibid.

[30] Co-operative News, 1 June, 1940, p16.

[31] Co-operative News, 7 September, 1940, p5.

[32] Co-operative News, 5 October, 1940, p1. (My Emphasis).

[33] For a discussion of censorship in World War Two see STAMMERS, N (1983) Civil Liberties in Britain During the 2nd World War (London).

[34] Co-operative News, 23 October, 1943, p1.; Co-operative News, 17 March, 1945, p1.

[35] REEVES, J (1938) 'Advance Democracy', The Wheatsheaf, October, pVIII.

[37] World Film News, October, 1938, p268.

[38] ibid. A copy of the film is preserved at the National Film Archive. Descriptions of the film are given in: 'Advance Democracy' op cit and HOGENKAMP, B, op cit pp187–188.

[39] REEVES, J (1944) A Century of Rochdale Co-operation (London). A copy of the film is preserved at the National Film Archive.

J H POYSER: LOCAL CO-OPERATIVE FILMS

The co-operative movement's adoption of film and film-making to aid in the expression of its commercial, political and cultural ideals, must be appreciated as a challenge to the hegemony of commercial cultural practices. The activities and propaganda of J Reeves and F H W Cox offer the most overt examples. There remains another area of 'alternative' film-making to be explored, 'amateur' films, produced by the members of co-operative societies, detailing the local development, and day to day business, of co-operation. Advances in 'sub-standard' technology had ensured the increasing widespread availability of equipment, and, literally allowed for the 'access to the means of production' by workers' organisations.[1]

In 1923 Eastman Kodak (film stock) and Bell and Howell (technology) had standardised sub-standard film stock to 16mm, although 17.5mm and 9.5mm formats did linger on for some years, and the availability of reversal film reduced further the cost of film-making.[2]

The necessary technology was well within the means of a co-operative education committee, and, as a 'booming' hobby, an experienced ciné-photographer could usually be found (as had been the case with Frank Cox at the London Co-operative Society. See chapter 4). A notable propagandist for 'Local Co-operative Films' was J H Poyser, a member of the education committee of the Long Eaton Co-operative Society, in Derbyshire. He had commenced experiments in 16mm silent film-making in the Summer of 1934, and the experience had 'proved convincingly that the sub-standard film is a popular and most fruitful medium of co-operative propaganda, education and entertainment'.[3] Four subjects were completed: *Hospital Carnival*; *The Town's Municipal Works*; *Building the Co-operative*

Emporium; and *Co-operative Milk*; the latter film 'showing the progress of milk from the cows grazing on the society's farm, through the dairy processes and distribution, to the member's tea-table'.[4] Produced in the sunshine months of the summer, a programme of exhibition was commenced in the winter, the traditional period of society propaganda activities. Over 60 two-hour shows were given, which were enlivened with short comic films specially purchased for the purpose. Poyser was careful to equate successful propaganda with enjoyment and entertainment, determining that 'Actually about 80% of the programme is 'what the audience wants'; the remaining 20% is made up of co-operative education and propaganda'.[5] He declared the education committee satisfied with that 20% propaganda which was reaching people to whom the Society could not otherwise appeal: 'We have found it attracts the young people between 18-25, who are bored stiff by co-operative speakers and will not attend either meetings or choir concerts'.[6] An element of its drawing power was the evident attraction 'of seeing yourself or your friends on the screen'.[7]

The education committee was eager to continue its support of the venture and four more projects were commissioned for the 1935 season. Production also became more ambitious with the proposal for a fictional subject. The popular *Hospital Carnival* became an annual project, and with it were completed *Co-operative Bread*, *Happy School Days* which included a short colour sequence of Jubilee Day, and the fictional *Spending The Divi*.[8] The latter film, showing the trials and trouble of an unemployed man and his family, and acted by society members, was intended to draw attention 'to the advantages of co-operation, dividend, collective life insurance, and the new emporium'.[9]

In 1936 the 'news reel' idea was adopted, with a film incorporating seven months in the life and activities of the local co-operative society and the town. 'News' items included a performance in the town by the CWS Tobacco Factory Band, Co-operators' Day festivities, the crowning of the Carnival Queen (a co-operative girl clerk), and the opening of a new branch store. Advertising films were attempted with a three and a half minute short promoting ladies shoes, which was conveniently exhibited next to the new film examining the society's cobblers. A particularly well received title was *The Travel Picture* about the society's mobile delivery van, considered 'twenty minutes of co-operative propaganda and education, a countryside panorama and a local geography lesson at the same time'.[10] The film depicts a typical day's round for the mobile hardware van, serving a rural community with lim-

Filming the Travel Picture (1936)

ited access to the local co-operative store, and incorporated an innovative 'subjective camera technique' whereby the audience were placed in the position of the mobile van, and which had been achieved by the cameraman valiantly strapping himself onto the moving vehicle. In 1936 the society purchased a 16mm sound projector to further its propaganda activities, and Poyser was gratified to discover that his own local films, all silent, were as well received as the professionally made sound films presented on the same programme. Sixty film shows were given between October 1936 and February 1937, and the following expenditures were incurred: film hire, £31 7s. 6d; film production, £40; transport, £14; venue hire and advertising, £17; and printing £22 5s. 6d. That giving an average cost per show of £2, and considered acceptable by the education committee for the valuable propaganda achieved.[11]

Poyser kept abreast of technical developments and 'talkie' films in colour were first attempted in 1937, with a *Mannequin Parade* film. Fictional subjects were further developed with *Saint Monday* (1937), illustrating how co-operative cleaning products and utensils can overcome the wash day blues, and *Holidays with Pay* (1938), which showed how the 'divi' could provide the funds for the family holiday to Skegness.[12]

Poyser devoted much energy promoting the use of 16mm film-making by local co-operative societies. He authored several articles, persistently raised the matter at co-operative conferences, and his 'successes' were widely reported in the co-operative press.[13] He maintained that 'Any society or education committee looking for an effective means of propaganda, advertising, or education would be well advised to consider the appeal of the "movies"', adding that 'local production is better than buying cinemas and using films produced in Hollywood or Elstree... Local scenes with local people in local activities have been the secret of success with films at Long Eaton'.[14] Giving the example of his own society, he felt that a combined programme of film production and exhibition, averaging £2 per show 'should be within the possibilities of medium sized societies'.[15] Furthermore, appreciative of the audience to whom he was appealing he added:

> There is the value to the trading side of the society to be considered. Here are comparative figures for the society's dairy trade during the period the co-operative milk film was being made and shown:
> cash sales - quarter ending April 14, 1934, £12,391
> cash sales - quarter ending April 13, 1935, £13,399
> An increase of over £1,000 per quarter (?).
> Here is something refreshingly and successfully different from standing on a platform bleating for loyalty.[16]

Poyser was not a lone voice in the crusade, but, importantly, his was backed up with practical success. Both J Reeves and F H W Cox had been involved in producing 16mm films of society activities, however, their intention went beyond that, and each sought, albeit in a different manner, the creation of a co-operative film body producing education and propaganda films for the entire movement. However, their promotion and propaganda undoubtedly fuelled the general discussions regarding the local society's use of film. Elsewhere a 'marriage' between co-operative thespians (the movement sponsored many drama groups) and ciné enthusiasts had been advocated in 1933.[17] As equipment continued to be improved, and further reduced in price, the advocacy of 'co-operative film-making' became more regular. An open conference on films was held at the 1938 Co-operative Union Education Convention, stimulating much discussion. A long article appeared in the Co-operative News priming delegates for the coming debate.[18] The main discussion centred on the extension of the movement's film-making beyond trade publicity films. It was recognised that 'Films Sell Our Goods', but then asked 'Why Not Employ Them To Sell Principles?'.[19] Successful activity was alluded to at Long Eaton, Leicester, Stockton, Kettering and London, and it was appreciated that:

> Educational committees and publicity men are pressing strongly for the provision of films and equipment which will enable their society's to show the public not only how co-operative goods are made, but why they are made.[20]

However, readers were forcefully reminded of the lack of good propaganda films which was preventing enterprising societies from giving regular displays. Practical advice was shortly on hand with the appearance of a regular column in the Co-operative News entitled 'Films For Co-operators', which discussed 'the practical aspects of co-operative film-making and projection'.[21] The series ran to 13 instalments between May and November, 1938. Guidance and information were provided on suitable technology, electrical supply, achieving clear projection, film libraries, film-making 'tips', and coloured photography amongst other things.

Film production at Portsea Island Mutual Co-operative Society, 1936

In the event, the response by societies and members was patchy. Most societies were quite content to rely on national bodies like the CWS and NACEC to provide them with film shows. Where film-making was successfully undertaken there simultaneously existed the desire on behalf of the society, and the presence of an enthusiastic member, or more probably, a publicity manager with the necessary skills and inclination. That conflation, of course, lay behind the success at Long Eaton. However, similar 'fortunate' arrangements were found elsewhere.

Mr R Denny (camera) and the Leicester Co-op Society Film Unit (1938)

The publicity department of Portsea Island Mutual Co-operative Society (PIMCO - trading in the Portsmouth area) managed by Mr R Denny, purchased a 16mm ciné-camera and projector in September 1935. Immediately a PIMCO News Reel was commenced, the first edition including 'a variety of subjects connected with the society, such as the employees' outing, an interview with Neil McCorkell, the famous Hants cricketer who is also a PIMCO member; the opening at Lee-on-Solent of the society's forty-third branch - and so on'.[22] At the same time a longer film of the society's dairy at Portsmouth was made.

The initial screenings, supplemented by a cartoon and live entertainer, were described as 'extraordinarily successful'. The society appreciated in the new medium, a unique method by which to inform the new member:

> For this purpose a new film is in course of production, entitled *Behind the Scenes* which deals with all the various workshops and services of the Society which are not readily visible to the new member. It is hoped that this will prove an invaluable method of acquainting a new member with the full extent of the society's services.[23]

The PIMCO publicity film department was active up to the Second World War, periodically releasing a news reel, producing accounts of the society's bread and milk divisions which included animated sequences, fashion films and fictional subjects such as *The Key* (c1937), extolling the benefits of the 'mutuality saving's scheme'.

At the Bolton Co-operative Society, film-making was centred on the Pharmacy and Photographic Department at the Market Street store, under the guidance of Mr A Booth, manager. By the Summer of 1935, the Department was offering a full range of cinematographic services, which included a film library 'intended chiefly for guilds and circles [and which] will provide films, projector and all equipment necessary for a show'. [24] Initially, activity was concentrated on film display, with exhibition allied to co-operative education classes and promoting the business of the Excursion Department. In 1938 the Department achieved prominence with its film record of the Scarborough Congress, for which an award-winning amateur film-maker, G H F Higginson, was approached to participate. Further success was recorded with a colour film study of Bolton Wanderers Football Club, including footage of matches against Middlesborough and Everton, considered to be the first of its kind. The film was exhibited at a co-operative exhibition in the town in October 1938, where the society ensured that the huge audience 'attracted by the opportunity to see their football favourites on the screen will also see other films devoted to co-operative propaganda'.[25] Further subjects included a film of Bolton's centenary celebrations, a film commissioned by the local Air Raid Precautions (ARP) and a general film on Bolton Society's activities, with proposals for films on the society's laundry and bakery.[26] Mr Booth also assisted other local societies in their film projects, providing both a colour film record of the 1939 pageant at Manchester's Belle Vue Stadium, and the opening of a new super dairy in 1941, for the Manchester and Salford Co-operative Society.

Leicester Co-operative Society established its publicity film unit under the guidance of its new publicity manager, Mr R Denny, who had helped pioneer film making at PIMCO. In August 1936, it was announced that 'Leicester Society has acquired a complete 'talkie' film apparatus and projector, with which to record and show pictures of the many activities of the society', and it was claimed that 'Leicester Society is probably one of the first societies to venture into "sound" film production'.[27] The Leicester Co-operative Society News Reel, with narration by Mr Denny, was the first project undertaken, and annual coverage of the society's Penny Bank Gala became a feature of production. The 1937 'News Reel' included colour footage taken of the arrival of Father Christmas and Disney characters to open the society's Christmas Bazaar. *Old Friends Meet* (1937) was the obligatory 'milk and bread' film, and cartoons were also attempted.[28] The films proved useful propaganda with 20 film displays given in the Spring of 1938, appealing to 4,500 adults and 5,000 children.[29] Mr Denny's reputation was such that he was engaged to produce a film demonstrating co-operative educational activities for the Education Department of the Co-operative Union, to be called *The Playway to Co-operative Knowledge* (1938).[30] In October 1938 Denny left the Leicester Co-operative Society to take a post at the Leicester Co-operative Printing Society. Co-operative film-making at Leicester appeared to have ended at this point, illustrating the crucial importance to a society, interested in local co-operative film-making, of an available, qualified, enthusiast.

The existing evidence, which unfortunately is sparse and scattered, does indicate that films of local co-operative activities were quite widespread. However, the films and film-makers of Long Eaton, PIMCO and Leicester were especially notable, both for their apparent success, and their promotional energies. Films relating to other co-operative societies were made, and seemingly began in 1909, with a short record of Co-operative Gala Day festivities at Wishaw, Scotland. It is often difficult to determine which films were produced co-operatively, by members or employees, or alternatively commissioned from local producers. For the record it is worthwhile to conclude with a list of co-operative societies, and member organisations, for which films were made:

> Barnsley British, Birkenhead, Birmingham, Blackpool, Bolton, Burslem, Coalville, Colchester, Cowdenbeath, Co-operative Women's Guild, Dartford, Dewsbury, Gillingham, Glasgow, Grays, Guildford, Ipswich, Kettering, Leicester, Leeds, Lochgelly, London, Long Eaton, Middlesborough, Newcastle, Nottingham, Nuneaton, Peterborough, PIMCO, Royal Arsenal, South Suburban, St Cuthburts, Stockport, Woodcraft Folk [31]

NOTES

[1] Without wishing to appear too deterministic, the progress of the Workers' Film Movement was dependent on cheaper, non-professional equipment. For a study of a leading workers' film group see : DENNET, T (1979) 'England : The (Workers) Film and Photo League' in Photography/Politics : One, pp100-117.

[2] Zimmermann, PR (1988) 'Professional Results With Amateur Ease' in Film History, September/October, pp267-281.

[3] POYSER, JH (1935) 'Local Co-operative Films' in The Producer, August, pp247-248.

[4] 'Local Co-operative Films', op cit p247.; POYSER, JH 'Twelve Months' Cinema Education' in The Co-operative Productive Review, pp185-186. Production details differ slightly in these two accounts. In the former the 'Emporium' film is dated as 1935, in the latter as 1934.

[5] 'Local Co-operative Films', op cit.

[6] 'Twelve Months' Cinema Education', op cit p186.

[7] ibid.

[8] 'Local Co-operative Films', op cit p247. Films detailing a society's milk and bread provision soon established themselves as the 'classic' subjects of co-operative film-making. The films delighted in taking the audience from the society's farm, through the whole chain of processes, to the final delivery of the pint or loaf, by the society, to the doorstep. A particularly representative example was Coalville Society's film *Progress* (1944), which presents the society's farm, dairy, bakery, the various departments of the Emporium, several of the branch stores, and even allows us to witness 'divi' day. All in 44 minutes.

[9] 'Local Co-operative Films', op cit p248.

[10] POYSER, JH (1937) 'Co-operators Should Be Shot' in The Producer, February, pp48-49. In the 1980s the 'Travel Picture' was given a voice-over narration, provided by the actual driver of the vehicle.

[11] Co-operative News, 3 April, 1937, p10.

[12] The Producer, July, 1937, p200.; The Co-operative News, 30 April, 1938, p11 provides a detailed description of the making of 'Saint Monday'; Co-operative News, 2 July, 1938, p3.

[13] As well as the above references see, for instance, The Wheatsheaf, November, 1934, p169; The Wheatsheaf, January, 1936, p2.; Co-operative Union Annual Congress Report, 1937, pp460-461.
[14] 'Local Co-operative Films', op cit p248.
[15] Co-operative News, 3 April, 1937, p10.
[16] 'Local Co-operative Films', op, cit p248. (My query).
[17] LAMMING, GN (1933) Co-operators as Film Actors, The Millgate, September, p691-692.
[18] Co-operative News, (Special Supplement), 9 April, 1938,
[19] ibid.
[20] ibid.
[21] Co-operative News, 7 May, 1938, p4.
[22] The Producer, November, 1935, p335. In a later article Denny states that film activities commenced at PIMCO in 1934. See Co-operative News, 5 November, 1938, p9. A collection of PIMCO films are preserved at the Wessex Sound and Film Archive.
[23] ibid.
[24] Co-operative News, 22 June, 1935, p9. It is probable that Mr Booth was the anonymous 'expert' behind the 'Films for Co-operators' column in the Co-operative News, already referred to.
[25] Co-operative News, 22 October, 1938, p3.
[26] Co-operative News, 3 December, 1938, p11
[27] Co-operative News, 22 August, 1936, p1. A collection of Leicester Co-operative Society films are preserved at the East Anglia Film Archive.
[28] Co-operative News, 4 December, 1937, p5.
[29] Co-operative News, 9 April, 1938, p5.
[30] Co-operative News, 13 August, 1938, p1.; Co-operative News, September 10, 1938, p9.
[31] In compiling this list I do not claim to be comprehensive. Rather, I intend to give an indication of the extent of co-operative society film-making in the period up to the 1960s.

The Blackpool Society's Jubilee News Theatre, 1938

HORACE MASTERMAN AND CO-OPERATIVE CINEMAS

In the introduction I briefly examined the three basic attitudes expressed by the labour movement to the cinema: Moralistic; Libertarian and Marxist. The provision of conventional cinema entertainment by retail co-operative societies best exemplifies the libertarian position. A study of the cinema industry by Dr R S Edwards of the Co-operative Union Central Board, in April 1937, concluded that:

> The people responsible for the great majority of cinema visits are potential if not actual co-operators. They go because they enjoy this form of entertainment... The conclusion must be accepted, therefore, that the cinema habit is sufficiently widespread among the working population to make this at least a possible field of co-operative enterprise.[1]

It must be conceded that supporters of that view usually allied it with the rather more fanciful idea that the movement should enter into commercial film production (and by implication distribution), to ensure that films portraying suitable ideological themes were made available to working audiences. For instance, co-operators were asked to 'imagine only what the co-operative outlook could have done with the themes of such films as *The Informer, Ours Alone*, and *Mutiny on the Bounty* - not to mention the subtly anti-co-operative *Things To Come*.[2] The local society, knowing full-well that the movement was not about to embark on feature film production, was forced into the more pragmatic position of considering its members leisure interests. Aware that 'the cinema-going habit was an essential feature of working class life' [3], a small number of societies established a new trading department, a cinema.

The value of film to a voluntary organisation had been appreciated well before the First World War. In February 1914, a Co-operative News editorial had asked: 'The Cinema. Should It Be Used For Co-operative Purposes?'.[4] The anonymous author perceived in the cinema a means of 'attracting the masses - young and old - in a way that would enable them to obtain knowledge, and at the same time be vastly entertained'. In that writer's view, the cinema was valuable to the co-operative movement in three inter-related ways: It could be used to induce audiences to become members of the Co-op, an important consideration to a voluntary organisation; it was a means of educating members about their business and about the benefits of co-operation; and it was unrivalled as the entertainment choice of the masses. Those three attributes were further emphasised later in the article, and a note of warning was introduced, when it was stated that the purpose of the cinema for the movement would be 'that of entertainment, education and social contact. If we do not make use of it, it will remain in the hands of other people to detract from our own forms of entertainment'. That combative tone was reflective of the co-operative movement's oppositional stance within the British economy, and its preparedness to confront the commercial, political and cultural values of capitalism.

The illusion to both the leisure and material needs of the co-operative community became an important feature of the debate as it developed in the inter-war period. Earlier, echoing the motivations of the original Rochdale Pioneers, it had been advocated that 'we should provide our own amusements, our own forms of social enjoyment. And our amusements and social enjoyments should be as pure as should be the food and clothes we supply for our material needs'.[5] Two decades later, W Henry Brown, who did much to promote the idea of co-operatively owned cinemas, wished to see the organisation of the 'amusements of our members. They come to the stores for their daily fare; why not supply their evening pleasures?'[6]

The local Co-op Hall had proved a convenient site for early film exhibition, which had been based on itinerant showmen. For instance, Henry Hibbert held a show at the Co-op Hall, Bingley, on the 22 February 1900.[7] Similarly, before the Great War, the Co-op Hall at Crewe became a regular venue for Arthur Hand and Son, and was known locally as 'Hand's Kino'.[8] Following the 1909 Cinematograph Act many co-operative societies licensed their premises for cinema exhibition, with particularly strong representation in the North of England.[9]

However, there gradually developed a more considered and permanent response by some retail co-operative societies. Indicative of that was the celebrated activity of Horace Masterman at the Dewsbury Pioneers' Industrial Society. For nearly 30 years the society's Pioneer Cinema was managed by Masterman, a man of exceptional energy and ability. The Pioneer Cinema had been established in September 1922, and was located within the society's Central Premises. It had first been used for cinema exhibition at least as early as 1909, when it regularly screened pictures provided by A O Andrews of Batley.[10] The Hall was refurbished in 1922, and exhibition was directly assumed by the society. Shortly after that date a cafe became a popular addition. Following the advent of the 'talkies', the Pioneer was further remodelled, and wired for sound by Western Electric in January 1931, with a seating capacity in excess of 1,500.[11] For three decades the cinema made a substantial contribution to the society's profits, which for the financial year of 1925, had been £1,972, despite the fact that the society had determined that the ticket prices would be less then those charged at other cinemas in the district.[12]

There is little doubting that Horace Masterman had a large part to play in the success of the Pioneer. He was a popular character and would himself occasionally provide live entertainment with a display of conjuring before the main programme.[13] His particular talent seemed to lie in his enterprising approach to publicity. In 1936 he won the national prize offered by Radio Pictures for the best exploitation in this country of *The Little Minister*. In his publicity scheme, Masterman demonstrated the advantages belonging to a co-operative cinema manager. His approach included special shop window displays, the production of 60,000 milk bottle disks which carried his special shopping week slogan 'Little Minister Shopping Week - Let the Co-op Minister to your Needs', and appeals to patrons through the microphone, circulars, handbills, posters and the press. In addition, a special arrangement was made to forward to Katharine Hepburn, the star of the film, a selection of letters from Dewsbury film-goers.[14]

Horace Masterman's publicity campaigns continued to reap dividends and reach the headlines. In 1938 his publicity scheme for Capra's *Lost Horizon* won the award of merit offered by Columbia Pictures, and his promotion of *Fire Over England* (1937), *Green Pastures* (1937), and *The Drum* (1938) attracted considerable local attention.[15]

Another innovation appears to have been brought to a halt by the Second World War. Literally on the eve of the war, it was reported that Masterman was making a film called *Sports of Dewsbury*, which would be shown at the Pioneer Cinema in October 1939.[16] Unfortunately the film does not appear to have survived. During that period Masterman's remaining energies were spent on civil duties, as Dewsbury Society prepared itself to face the Nazi on-slaught:

> Mr Horace Masterman, Manager of the Pioneer Cinema, has been appointed ARP Officer, and that the society is ready for anything that might happen is due in no small measure to his energy and ability.[17]

With the return of peace, Masterman was free again to concentrate all his attention on the cinema business. In February 1949 he inaugurated the first Junior Film Club in the co-operative movement, whereby '1,000 young members, charged 6d, enjoyed a two-hour show. The club was not run on a profit-making basis but for the benefit of the youngsters'.[18] The society did not lose the opportunity of screening films showing the merits of the movement, and some were included in the programme. Twenty-five lucky children from the first show were given a trip to Leeds to meet 'Dick Barton' and see his new film.[19] CinemaScope was installed at the first opportunity in February 1954, part of the general attempt to stave off the decline in audiences. Despite his conjuring skills, Masterman was no magician, and he succumbed to the inevitable. The Pioneer was leased to the Essoldo circuit in September 1960, ignobly seeing out its days as the Tatler Cinema specialising in adult films. Masterman remained at the society as its Catering Manager.

The success of Horace Masterman at Dewsbury elevated him into the position of 'unofficial' cinema expert of the co-operative movement. In that capacity he acted as film advisor to the nearby Horbury Society, and also the Scunthorpe Society, both of which operated cinemas. Further, he was called upon to act as technical advisor in the fitting-up of Blackpool Society's Jubilee News Theatre in 1938. He was well-liked in the trade, where his flair and ability were appreciated. After the war he was regularly elected to the Chair of the Leeds and District Branch of the Society of Cinema Managers.

A prize-winning window display in the Dewsbury Campaign to promote The Little Minister

Generally, co-operative cinemas were more in evidence in the North of England [20], with particular concentrations in the North East and West Riding/Lancashire area. Co-operative cinemas were operated by the following societies: Billington and Whally (near Blackburn); Clitheroe; Kirkham (Lancashire); Mossley (Yorkshire); Poynton-with-Worth (Cheshire); Middlestown (Yorkshire); Meltham and Meltham Mills (near Huddersfield); and Long Buckby (Northants); in addition to the three previously mentioned. In many instances the local society had sought to provide cinema entertainment where none had previously existed, and were therefore often found in small towns. The chief exceptions to that were Dewsbury and Scunthorpe, which successfully faced considerable local competition well into the 1950s.[21]

The reaction of the commercial cinema trade to this incursion into their business by the co-operative movement, is instructive. Primarily, local cinema proprietors were irked at the practice of co-operative cinemas paying dividends on admission. The Co-operative News gleefully recorded the nervous comment of an Oldham exhibitor who declared 'Heaven forbid the time will come when the Lancashire mill hand will go to the local cinema and ask for "two nine-pennies and dividend check"'.[22] The trade undoubtedly feared the competitiveness of co-op cinemas who were able to offer that inducement. Councillor W Woolstencroft, Director and Manager of the South and East Lancashire Branch of the Co-operative Exhibitors Association, writing in the Kine Weekly, fully appreciated the threat to the capitalist tenets of the business, and his own privileged position, when he declared that 'Profit from private businesses go to the investor shareholders. Those from Co-ops go to the customer'.[23]

At the end of World War II there was considerable comment in the trade press regarding proposed further activities by the movement. At times, there was a genuine fear in the film trade that the movement was planning to establish a cinema circuit. Comments emanating from the movement, apparently substantiating that fact, were nervously reported in the trade papers. A headline in the Daily Film Renter warned that the 'London Co-op Wants Big Cine Circuit'. The concern followed a speech by the noted left-wing theorist G D H Cole at a meeting organised by the London Co-operative Society Education Committee. Cole had stipulated that:

> It is no use the Co-operative Movement splashing in the kinema trade unless they make a big splash, for it means

competition with great existing kinema chains and monopolies. We must have control of a great chain of kinemas or producing agencies so that we have a chance of showing a particular kind of film.[24]

The great wave of socialist euphoria that swept Britain towards the end of the war, with enthusiastic calls for widespread nationalisation, no doubt further added to the unease of the industry. By April 1945, the Kine Weekly was declaring a 'Co-op Circuit Menace', and feared 'the possibility that the Co-operative Movement would invade the kinema exhibitors field'.[25] Less than a month later, the trade's unease had reached paranoid levels. 'Co-ops Could Be Biggest Circuit' was a headline in The Cinema, in May 1945. It quoted J Mather of the South and East Lancashire Branch of the CEA, whose view of the movement was that 'If it embarked upon cinema enterprise it could be build (sic) up bigger circuits that (sic) G-B, Odeon and ABC... With the wealth that they had they could buy up the present major circuits'.[26]

For the more sober-minded exhibitor, the serious threat lay with the CWS, and its dispensation towards developing a cinema chain. Councillor Woolstencroft, in his article for Kine Weekly previously referred to, realised that, and warned that 'As Kinema owners don't let us underestimate the menace'. He pointed to the financial trading strength of the CWS, which at that time had disposable assets of £22 million and further reserves of £29 million. He ominously noted the movement's establishment of the Peoples' Entertainment Society which, within twelve months of its founding in 1942, had purchased two theatres. The concerns of the conventional industry reached a ludicrous height in the Summer of 1946, with the establishment of the National Film Association by the broad labour movement. That alliance of Labour Party, TUC and co-operative movement was reported to be considering the purchase of a Scottish cinema circuit and, even more improbably, the Kine Weekly stated that 'Reports from Scotland indicate that plans are well advanced for putting up film studios'.[27] Not surprisingly, nothing materialised and, when it transpired that the majority Labour Government was not about to appropriate the cinemas for the workers, panic subsided.

This survey of the film exhibition activities of the co-operative movement emphasises once again the possibility of 'alternative' practices within the cinema industry. Considerable attention has been devoted to the film-making activities of the inter-war labour movement, however, it is necessary to stress that commercial exhibition was not ignored, and indeed a modest element of success can be conceded. Co-operative cinemas did not ruthlessly equate entertainment with profit. Societies establishing cinemas sought to provide, primarily, a service to their members and, in addition, that investment reflected the movement's appreciation of its community responsibility. It is clear that the film trade saw the development as a threat to its position, and sought ways of emasculating the activity. No great chain of co-operative cinemas serving the people was ever built. However, a number of communities, such as Horbury, Dewsbury and Blackburn, were able to enjoy a evening's entertainment in their own cinema, and to the benefit of their own society.

The classical façade of Blackpool Co-operative Society's Emporium. The Jubilee News Theatre occupied the top floor, 1938

NOTES

[1] EDWARDS, R.S (1937) 'The Cinema and Co–operative Prospects' in the Co–operative Review, April, pp108–111. For his statistics Edwards relies on the famous study conducted by Simon Rowson in 1934, into the British film industry.

[2] MOIR, SEL (1937) 'Co–operative Films – When?' in The Millgate, January, pp200–201.

[3] RYALL, T (1986) Alfred Hitchcock and the British Cinema (Chicago) p37.

[4] Co–operative News, 28 February, 1914, pp268–269.

[5] ibid.

[6] The Co–operative Official, 1936, p139.

[7] MELLOR, GJ (1971) Picture Pioneers (Newcastle) p22.

[8] ibid. p41.

[9] For a discussion of the Movement's dominance in the north of England see SOUTHERN J (1993) 'Co–operation in the North West of England, 1919–1939' in The Journal of Regional and Local Studies, Summer, pp68–83.

[10] Picture Pioneers, op cit. p29.

[11] Co–operative News, 10 January, 1931, p3.

[12] Co–operative News, 12 December, 1925, p1.

[13] The Dewsbury Reporter, 7 April, 1989, p10.

[14] Co–operative News, 7 March, 1936, p6.; The Producer, March, 1936, p82.

[15] Co–operative News, 11 September, 1937, p6.; Co–operative News, 6 November, 1937, p6.; Co–operative News, 5 February, 1938, p1.; Co–operative News, 18 February, 1939, p11

[16] Co–operative News, 2 September, 1939, p3.

[17] Co–operative News, 30 September, 1939, p6.

[18] The Producer, April, 1949, p26.

[19] ibid.

[20] See Note 9.

[21] A more detailed survey of Co–op cinemas can be found in BURTON, A (1993) 'The Peoples' Cinemas: The Picture Houses of the Co–operative Movement' in Picture House, no.19, pp3–13.

[22] Co–operative News, 16 June, 1945, p8.

[23] Kine Weekly, 24 May, 1945, p5.

[24] Daily Film Renter, 21 February, 1945, p3.

[25] Kine Weekly, 5 April, 1945, p13.
[26] The Cinema, 2 May, 1945, p31.
[27] Kine Weekly, 22 August, 1946, p1.

CONCLUSION

This study has brought to light the diversity of approaches to film and film-making exhibited by the co-operative movement during the period of cinema's dominance as a mass medium. That diversity is readily understandable when it is recalled that at its height, at the end of World War II, the movement consisted of approximately 1,200 independent retail societies, claimed a membership approaching 10 million, and held a retail market share of nearly 12%. Representing those societies were national, federal organisations like the Co-operative Union and the CWS, who had the difficult task of responding to demands that were often conflicting and contradictory. With respect to film that situation was evident in the late 1930s when societies could choose from two co-operative film services, one sponsored by the Co-operative Union in association with the CWS, the other offered by the National Association of Co-operative Education Officials.

At the regional level, local rivalries could seemingly interfere with the development of co-ordinated activity. London was served by the two largest co-operative societies, London, trading north of the Thames, and Royal Arsenal, trading to the south. As we have seen, both societies extensively supported film-making, yet there was little willingness to co-ordinate their resources and to collaborate. That was undoubtedly a combination of traditional rivalries between the two societies, and the rather different approaches to film promoted by Joseph Reeves (RACS), who favoured production on 35mm, and Frank Cox (LCS), who championed 16mm direct-sound recording. Whatever, the result was a dissipation of energies and resources, for what was, in the final reckoning, the same ultimate aim.

Some film critics on the Left have been dismissive of the co-operative movement's achievements with respect to film. Paul Rotha, the noted documentary film-maker and historian, writing immediately after World War II, considered that the socialists' use of film had been a failure, and, concentrating on the CWS' advertising films, that the co-operative movement's contribution had been dismal. Such an estimation was unfair, and I would hope that this introductory survey of the co-operative movement's use of film goes some way towards contesting that judgement. Rotha's view-point ignores the very diversity of demands placed on the film

Production of Counter Courtesy (1947), produced by Orion Picture Corp for the SCWS

medium by the movement, which sought to address commercial, political and cultural objectives. In the outcome, that very diversity, represented by the publicity films of the CWS, the educational strategies pursued by Joseph Reeves, political film-making undertaken by Frank Cox, members' films produced at numerous societies, and the entertainment enjoyed by numerous co-operators in their own cinemas, led to a surprising breadth of film activity. I would conclude, that in the final analysis, the co-operative movement's achievement with film was commendable. I sincerely hope that audiences will once again enjoy and appreciate the fruits of all that co-operative endeavour when a selection of films are screened during the Festival of Films on Co-operation in 1994.

BIBLIOGRAPHY

ATTFIELD, J
WITH LIGHT OF KNOWLEDGE
A hundred years of education in the Royal Arsenal Co-operative Society, 1877 – 1977, London and West Nyack, RACS/Journeyman Press, 1981.

BONNER, A
BRITISH CO-OPERATION
Manchester, Co-operative Union, 1970.

BURTON, A
'THE PEOPLE's CINEMAS: The Picture Houses of the Co-operative Movement'
Picture House no 19, Winter 1993/94.

COLE, GDH
A CENTURY OF CO-OPERATION
Manchester, Co-operative Union, 1944.

HOGENKAMP, B
DEADLY PARALLELS
Film and the Left in Britain 1929 – 39, London, Lawrence and Wishart, 1986.

MACPHERSON, D (ed)
BRITISH CINEMA
Traditions of Independence, London, BFI, 1980.

JONES, SG
THE BRITISH LABOUR MOVEMENT AND FILM
1918 – 39, London, RKP, 1987.

REDFERN, P
THE NEW HISTORY OF THE CWS
London, JM Dent and Sons, 1938.

REEVES, J
A CENTURY OF ROCHDALE CO-OPERATION
1844-1944, London, Lawrence and Wishart, 1944.

RICHARDSON, SIR W
THE CWS IN WAR AND PEACE
1938 – 1976, Manchester, Co-operative Wholesale Society Ltd, 1977.

RYAN, T
'THE NEW ROAD TO PROGRESS': The Use and Production of Films by the Labour Movement 1929-39
in CURRAN, J and PORTER, V
BRITISH CINEMA HISTORY
London, Weidenfeld and Nicholson, 1983.

YEO, S (ed)
NEW VIEWS OF CO-OPERATION
London, Routledge, 1988.

For a recent general appraisal of the movement since 1945 see:
CONSUMER CO-OPERATION IN THE UNITED KINGDOM
1945-1993
Journal of Co-operative Studies (special edition) No 79, February 1994.